Cambridge Elements ≡

Elements in Public Policy
edited by
M. Ramesh
National University of Singapore (NUS)
Michael Howlett
Simon Fraser University, British Columbia
Xun WU
Hong Kong University of Science and Technology
Judith Clifton
University of Cantabria
Eduardo Araral
National University of Singapore (NUS)

DISRUPTED GOVERNANCE

Towards a New Policy Science

Kris Hartley
The Education University of Hong Kong

Glen David Kuecker
DePauw University, Indiana

CAMBRIDGE
UNIVERSITY PRESS

University Printing House, Cambridge CB2 8BS, United Kingdom

One Liberty Plaza, 20th Floor, New York, NY 10006, USA

477 Williamstown Road, Port Melbourne, VIC 3207, Australia

314–321, 3rd Floor, Plot 3, Splendor Forum, Jasola District Centre,
New Delhi – 110025, India

103 Penang Road, #05–06/07, Visioncrest Commercial, Singapore 238467

Cambridge University Press is part of the University of Cambridge.

It furthers the University's mission by disseminating knowledge in the pursuit of
education, learning, and research at the highest international levels of excellence.

www.cambridge.org
Information on this title: www.cambridge.org/9781009125680
DOI: 10.1017/9781009127868

First published 2022

A catalogue record for this publication is available from the British Library.

ISBN 978-1-009-12568-0 Paperback
ISSN 2398-4058 (online)
ISSN 2514-3565 (print)

Disrupted Governance

Towards a New Policy Science

Elements in Public Policy

DOI: 10.1017/9781009127868
First published online: Feburary 2022

Kris Hartley
The Education University of Hong Kong
Glen David Kuecker
DePauw University, Indiana
Author for correspondence: Kris Hartley hartley@eduhk.hk

Abstract: This Element explores the uncertain future of public policy practice and scholarship in an age of radical disruption. Building on foundational ideas in policy sciences, we argue that an anachronistic instrumental rationalism underlies contemporary policy logic and limits efforts to understand new policy challenges. We consider whether the policy sciences framework can be reframed to facilitate deeper understandings of this anachronistic epistemic, in anticipation of a research agenda about epistemic destabilization and contestation. The Element applies this theoretical provocation to environmental policy and sustainability, issues about which policymaking proceeds amid unpredictable contexts and rising sociopolitical turbulence that portend a liminal state in the transition from one way of thinking to another. The Element concludes by contemplating the fate of policy's epistemic instability, anticipating what policy understandings will emerge in a new system, and questioning the degree to which either presages a seismic shift in the relationship between policy and society.

Keywords: critical studies, environmental studies, public administration, public policy, sustainability

ISBNs: 9781009125680 (PB), 9781009127868 (OC)
ISSNs: 2398-4058 (online), 2514-3565 (print)

Contents

1 Introduction

The convergence of complex, interconnected, synchronous, and intractable problems is the salient existential challenge of the twenty-first century. Examples are pandemics, climate change, economic inequality, social disenfranchisement, and global insecurity – and, more importantly, the way they interact to magnify the collective impacts. A central premise of this Element is that the old ways of thinking about public policy have generated the conditions for such problems to emerge and have a poor record of resolving them. Further, the committed application of old ways of thinking, even when refashioned around novel technologies, institutional reform, and policy change, accelerate problem convergence. This Element critically interrogates the epistemic roots of policymaking as understood by existing theories, with the aim of illuminating new theoretical space for the emergence of a twenty-first-century policy epistemic in scholarship and practice. Our normative orientation is a critical perspective, informed by the Frankfurt School and postcolonial studies, on the dominance of policy narratives that privilege certain ideologies, serve power, and perpetuate crisis conditions despite their claims to the contrary. Our novelty – a call to action for scholarship in public policy – is an examination of how the COVID-19 pandemic is a temporally condensed preview of longer-evolving crises like climate change, and how such crises render the old policy thinking anachronistic during a liminal moment in systemic transition. The audience for this call includes not only those who embrace critical policy studies but also scholars and practitioners in multiple geographies and contexts who operate under mainstream understandings of public policy.

This Element focuses on the epistemics of policy rather than on the ontology of policy, as the former relates more directly to our argument about instrumental rationalism. At the same time, we acknowledge that ontological factors cannot be ignored because they determine how public policy itself is conceptualized. As part of this acknowledgment, we propose a particular definition of policy to observe how it has become anachronistic and to consider what happens to policy when it enters the liminal state of a soft collapse transition. We derive our definition from the field of translation studies, as elaborated in Berger and Esguerra's (2017) *World Politics in Translation*. We proceed with an understanding of policy as the step between what needs to be done and the actual doing; a translation between thought and the "real world" where policy provides instructions, guardrails, and rule sets. This translation occurs within the context of actors, ideas, and institutions that shape content and mediate implementation (Clarke et al., 2015). As policy produces, sustains, and reproduces itself and its rule sets, it emerges as one of several determinants of power relations and

influences how social, political, economic, and cultural practices become hegemonic forms of "common sense." Like other expressions and conduits of power,
policy is limited, unstable, and in many cases contested due to its divergence
and fluidity. While "policy" as a broad and often amorphous concept defies
attempts at definitional essentialization, we maintain that policy's multiple
paths, instabilities, and contestations are settings in which hegemonic rule sets
can still take hold. Based on this argument, this Element contends that technocratic rationalism emerged in the twentieth century as the dominant mechanism
for policy's translation between abstraction and the real world, and that the
perpetuation of this technocratic rule set into the twenty-first century has made
policy anachronistic in concept and practice. This anachronism renders technocratic rationalism increasingly dysfunctional as the "sense" in common sense.
As such, we ask what happens to policy's translation function when systemic
context enters the liminal state of a soft collapse. Our cautionary proposition is
that anachronistic policy is a poor translator in this liminal state.

In probing the evident failures of public policy to address complex problems,
an influential line of scholarly criticism holds that policymaking has been
unduly influenced by instrumental rationalism.[1] The allegation is that instrumental rationalism is mismatched with complex problems because it sees only
what it can measure and fails to acknowledge the full range of problem
determinants, intensifiers, and their social constructions (Colebatch, 2018;
Turnbull, 2006). In this way, critics impugn instrumental rationalism not only
for failing to understand policy problems but also for exacerbating sociopolitical inequities and perpetuating power imbalances. Indeed, such criticisms have
been leveled for decades, within both critical policy studies and less mainstream
strands of public policy and administration. As minority voices in the field of
public policy, critical theorists resolutely disavow instrumental rationalism and
challenge the hegemony of its positivist epistemics. This critical studies scholarship often bears a normative mandate for the policy field to embrace con-
structivist, interpretivist, and discursive perspectives associated broadly with
critical theory.

This Element goes beyond this convincing but well-trodden argument about
instrumental rationalism. The basis of our provocation to prevailing understandings about and practices of policymaking is that the field is anachronistic. That

---

[1] For our definition of instrumental rationalism, see the Glossary. We define instrumental rationalism as the thought-system and accompanying rule set holding that discrete and targeted policy
interventions (as instruments or tools) can be successfully applied to problems expressed in
knowable and well-defined terms. We use the term instrumental rationalism, as against instrumental rationality, in reference to a normative logic around which the policy profession structures
its analytical thinking. If rationality is the act of being rational, rationalism is the epistemic rule set
and belief system that institutionalizes rationality.

is, ways of thinking about and doing public policy emerged from or were designed around the realities of twentieth-century problems, with the expectation that such problems could be managed if not solved. Only with the convergence of twenty-first-century problems – complex, interconnected, synchronous, and elusive of conclusive solutions – are the epistemic and practical shortcomings of a solutionist approach to policymaking exposed.

Mainstream scholarly efforts to determine the extent of policy success or failure have seldom considered the match between the dominant policy epistemic and the broader context of humanity's complex adaptive system. McConnell's (2010) study of policy success has been valuable for establishing frameworks for measurement but also reflects a dominant intellectual perspective that assumes policy's ways of thinking accord in concept and practice with the complex adaptive system in which policy is embedded. This perspective suggests either that policy assumes, anticipates, or works towards the equilibrium of the broader system, or that policy can stand detached from systemic context including that characterized by disequilibrium. Public policy and scholarly understandings of it thus lose their connection to reality as that reality slips into a bewildering state of wicked problems, destabilized epistemics, and ultimately soft collapse. As such, influential scholarly works concerning success and other aspects of policymaking were fit to context in their time but become increasingly anachronistic, as do the policies they study.

By retaining pre-crisis ways of thinking about problems and solutions, the policy field perpetuates a faulty epistemic, and society fails to avert its own overshoot of socio-ecological carrying capacities. The current manifestation of this phenomenon is a "soft" collapse (Kuecker 2020) in which some institutions (i.e., ways of thinking codified into policy practice) remain seemingly stable due to a resolute doubling-down on the vehicles – political and financial – that prop them up. The academic mainstream of public policy appears to be a partner in this effort by refitting its own anachronistic epistemic to new contexts; the fundamentals are argued by vestals of the old epistemic hearth to be sound if not canonical, in need only of better analytical tools, concepts, and frameworks. The foundations of enabling institutions are, to be fair, still considered by the mainstream to be fair targets for critique – but correctible by the same types of solutions that had always seemed to work for simpler problems erstwhile. With more complex tools, the profession in study and practice believes it can accomplish what it always has – but more quickly, efficiently, and effectively. The tragic inconvenience is that shifts in problem context often outpace policy evolution, compromising the immediate relevance of old epistemics to emergent crises. The consequent time lag engenders an anachronism that fails the new context of the twenty-first century and the "perfect storm" of convergent crises (i.e., ecological degradation, pandemics, and the folly of addressing them while protecting the systems and rule sets that benefit status quo interests).

We observe the anachronistic quality of modern policymaking not exclusively in its practical manifestation – instrumental rationalism – but also in an underlying epistemic that validates as a policy logic the concepts of "solutionism" and "problemacity"; both are reflected in Deweyian and Lasswellian pragmatism and more broadly in the problem orientation of the policy sciences tradition (Turnbull, 2006). The understanding of reality offered by this epistemic is disciplined by its frame of vision; when elements able to be measured are seen, the unseen is erased over time from a reality that is ultimately constructed for rhetorical or political purposes. Indeed, much of what is unseen by efforts to name and frame policy problems relates to context – a matter that theoretical approaches like the policy sciences framework attempt to address by measuring tangential properties (Cairney et al., 2019; Ascher, 1987). It is appropriate, however, to reflect not only on context but also on shifts of context; the scale of those shifts; and whether legacy epistemics fully capture the emergent complexities, uncertainties, and nuances of new contexts. Until the policy field sees the twenty-first century as a context shift, the old epistemic will continue to make sense while failing in practice – and scholars will continue to engage in handwringing about why better analytical tools, concepts, and frameworks make no larger difference. If society has indeed breached the threshold of a new context, it is fair to question whether this new era renders old styles of policy thinking anachronistic.

In making this provocation, we acknowledge the decades of literature about wicked problems, which have confronted technocratic hubris and prompted scholarly conversations about the ambiguities of policy context (Head, 2019; Peters, 2017; Scott, 1998; Rittel and Webber, 1973). Synchronous and interconnected crises are the wicked problems of the twenty-first century and deserve not merely a reform-minded and reworked epistemic framing but also an ontological reawakening that questions the very foundations of how society is structured and the role of policy (as authority or an organizing mechanism) within it. As such, public policy made relevant for the new context would not be public policy at all, in the way academics and practitioners now choose to understand it. Adherence to the notion of public policy as a logical system by which society organizes itself to solve collective problems is indicative of a soft rather than a hard collapse, because it leads to momentary illusions of stability and success made possible by superficial improvements to old thinking (e.g., through better and "bigger" data and their "smart" application). However, this reframing fails to forestall the irreversible destabilization of underlying systems and arguably accelerates it by obscuring or window-dressing negative effects that might otherwise be apparent enough to alarm society. Progress becomes, simply, a faster and cheaper way to do the wrong things.

Understanding the current era of public policy scholarship and practice as existing in this liminal state between old and new epistemics allows us to de-essentialize our critique of public policy in that we avoid reducing policy epistemics to a Platonic ideal; rather, we emphasize the prospects of freedom from old structures as made possible during periods of disruptive and large-scale transitions. In short, the policy field in a soft collapse–driven context shift is free from the old paradigm and its enabling structures, but their replacements are not yet sitting in a box at the front door. There is no imminent revolution after which the alternative is ceremoniously revealed. The liminal state is a lumbering era of disorder and noise, where truths are destabilized and discredited and the consequent epistemic confusion marks only the potential for liberation from the old paradigm. This state reflects Connolly's (2011) description of emergence as a "world of becoming" having "unnumerable, interacting open systems with differential capacities of self-organization set on different scales of time, agency, creativity, viscosity, and speed" (p. 25). Connolly (2013) sees emergence as a condition of late capitalism, whereas we see it as the in-between-ness of an unfolding collapse. The liminal state implies that the legitimacy of technocratic reasoning is undermined, and with it the moral and technical authority of policy experts and agents. Amid the noise of liminality and epistemic reshuffling, alternative policy epistemics have no less validity and thus an opportunity to emerge without the hindrances of legacy institutions and their tools of erasure. Eschewing a teleological approach, we argue that this process is no product of master planning or cynical capture by aggrieved parties, but a natural consequence of epistemic stasis and indeed rot. We seek to elucidate how the process materializes, so that opportunities for new theoretical development can be recognized. Our critique broadly concerns how the evolutionary product of Western Enlightenment thinking has precipitated one of the great follies of the modern social sciences – intellectual support for the technocratic solutionism that has dominated policy practice and mainstream policy scholarship.

This Element's argument is based more on practical realities than its deeply theoretical nature may make it appear. The cavalcade of totalizing and neocolonial post-WWII war policy projects – modernization, development, sustainability, and now smartness – reflect a long-running policy epistemic that has evolved in rhetoric if not concept and substance. To maintain its legitimacy through the twenty-first century, the old epistemic must rationalize and subdue complex problems while maintaining enough contextual stability to protect status quo political and economic systems and the interests that benefit from them. Despite this charge, whatever policy learning that emerged from addressing the twentieth century's wicked problems, including learning that might have prompted critical reflection on prevailing policy epistemics, might not be serving society well so far in the twenty-first century. On a global level, the COVID-19 crisis may be seen as a condensed version of the type of synchronous and interconnected disruptions that will emerge in the twenty-first century, and the ability of the wealthy and influential to insulate themselves from the impacts gives further effect to the illusion of stability held among those in power. The band plays on, even as the ship sinks.

The COVID-19 pandemic exhibits how twenty-first-century policy crises are not contained problems but converge with and exploit the vulnerabilities of multiple concurrent problems, leading to a cascade of failures that tips human systems into a series of soft collapses that can potentially precipitate an apocalyptic hard collapse; the imminence of collapse becomes the new system's context that frustrates solutionist policy logic. As the *res novae* emerging from a confluence of policy crises, the twenty-first century's perfect storm is composed of an onslaught of challenges that, to extend the metaphor, can be seen as frontal bands – arriving in waves, converging on one another, and multiplying the collective effects. Given these circumstances, the current moment is an existential flash point and should be recognized as such by policy practitioners and scholars. A post-pandemic policy epistemic is ripe for development, and this Element establishes the theoretical basis for how such a policy epistemic might be understood. Undertaking such work does not categorically dismiss the validity of existing scholarship, but it calls upon scholars to reframe it in potentially creative and even iconoclastic ways. The liminal state between epistemic regimes renders all scholarly understandings valid and none hegemonic, as any conceptualization of public policy has the potential to influence emergent understandings; a genuine epistemic shift breaks the path dependencies that privilege certain policy frames. A lingering question, then, is what emerges from this liminal state as the new context comes into focus; a new policy epistemic will not necessarily be the product of a totalizing dictate or even an organized effort. This emergence is a transition, more a process than an event, and takes time – potentially much of the twenty-first century. Society is at the starting point of this process, when difficult questions need to be asked about how society understands the fundamental essence of policymaking itself – whether as an epistemic, behavior, or value set. At this stage, the role of the pioneer scholar is to establish theoretical space for discussions about how the new epistemic emerges, and this Element advances this effort by exhibiting how that process might look. We thus heed calls by numerous scholars to proceed with an open mind; Turnbull's (2006) "epistemology of questioning" and

Homer-Dixon's (2006) "prospective mind," and system dynamicists preference for qualitative forecasting over predictive precision (Meadows, 1980, 2008) indicates that navigating the liminal state should be done with humility. We observe such caution in, for example, postulating that the anachronistic quality of policymaking and its mismatch for twenty-first-century problems may bear the severity if not the speed of the COVID-19 pandemic.

In considering the many pathways by which a new epistemic fills or redefines the gap vacated by the abandoned public policy anachronism, it is necessary to revisit the notion of public policy itself as a construct. Our proposition is that the new public policy will not simply be a reworking of existing public policy. Indeed, decades of scholarly reflection have led to a rigid essentialism – the view that public policy as an idea or behavior is conceptually reducible and Cartesian. As such, policy practice is anchored not only in the solutions and capabilities at hand but also in a dichotomous set of approaches bequeathed by rivalrous scholarly traditions: totalizing interventionism and measured incrementalism – with the latter still presuming "an instrumental approach directed by more or less clearly formulated intentions" (Turnbull, 2006, p. 12). These traditions, while representing opposite ends of a continuum, still share a focus on solutions – an approach itself anchored in the problem orientation of the policy sciences. In breaking with this orientation, a novel twenty-first-century policy epistemic would be focused not on solutionism but on some alternative that – by virtue of liminality and emergence – has no name, form, or even a vague signifier. Our proposal avoids framing terms like "precaution," "mitigation," and "preparedness," which are potentially problematic reflections of how fields like disaster risk reduction (Kuecker and Hartley, 2020) perpetuate instrumental-rationalist ways of thinking that put the soft in soft collapse. As such, a twenty-first-century epistemic is not merely the more intricate internalization of precaution and mitigation in existing policy logics and systems; this would, we argue, fail to capture the scale of the effort needed to see beyond instrumental rationalism. The new public policy is an emergent property that flows from soft collapse but is not knowable within the liminal state of transition and emergence. As such, the epistemic shift is not a revolution in the widely regarded sense, even though the act of seeing beyond rationalism can be considered equivalent in scale and consequence to an epistemic revolution. We do not necessarily call for such a revolution as an engineered effort, nor do we predict that revolution is the only way change happens. Rather, we argue that soft collapse is the "midwife of change" that creates the space for challenging epistemological structures and that kick-starts a transition with the liminal state being an intermediate step. The liminal state is thus characterized by epistemic noise and disciplinary territoriality, a faithful adherence to anachronistic ideas and emergent properties that elude classification but invite fresh theorization. Table 1 summarizes these ideas.

In developing this argument, this Element proceeds by introducing a case, outlining the aforementioned critical-analytical approach, and applying that approach to derive actionable policy insights. Section 2 introduces a case to explore our theoretical proposition of looming epistemic change. The case is the convergence of crises leading to soft collapse, as related primarily to sustainability and climate change but exacerbated by social conflict, economic precarity, state insecurity, and public health threats. As such, the case is focused not on a single policy domain but on problem convergence, reflecting our previous point about the realities of policy problems that spill over, interact, and synchronize. This approach also makes a methodological point: convergent crises are characterized by boundary jumping, rendering the standard single-case approach too myopic for the type of questions we ask in this Element. While single-case studies are indeed appropriate for answering certain questions, applying the approach to this argument would succumb to the same type of technocratic rationalism that we critique – indeed, our claims must be qualified and cautiously presented lest we indulge ourselves in a technocratic hubris that claims to know "the answer." Given our argument about emergence, liminality, and transition, we believe that conclusive statements are predictably difficult to make. In this Element, we hope to provide a sound basis for raising questions, pointing not only towards future research but also, potentially, a new subfield of policy studies focused on the evolution of the concept and governance more generally in a soft collapse setting.

Section 3 outlines the theoretical elements of our argument, including novelties and departures from mainstream scholarship. It traces the intellectual development of instrumental rationalism and the failures of its application not only to the complex and wicked policy challenges of the twentieth century but also to the synchronous and interconnected crises of the twenty-first century and their manifestation in an epistemically destabilizing soft collapse. It engages the policy sciences framework, Lasswellian pragmatism, and pragmatism in contemporary policy studies to review ideas about where solutionism and instrumental rationalism – and their underlying epistemic – have failed twentieth-century policy problems. In so doing, Section 3 aims to understand whether the policy sciences can retain their core theoretical foundations while adapting to a seismic transition in public policy – from epistemic anachronism to epistemic relevance in a soft collapse and emergent context. We maintain that such a course correction would need to recognize the autonomy of other knowledges, an argument we make in Section 3 using a postcolonial interpretation of how marginalized groups retain their autonomy through the de-othering power of alternative policy epistemics.

Table 1 Theoretical and practical dynamics of the old and new public policy epistemics

Theoretical dynamics		
Legacy (positivist)	Present (post-positivist; critical)	Liminality (epistemic tension)
Old epistemic	Dominant; supplement to practice	Anachronistic	Defensive; disciplinarily territorial
New epistemic	Marginal; incidental; situational	Iconoclastic; pesky; "playing from behind"	Assertive; emergent
Practical dynamics		
Legacy (solutionism; problemacity)	Present (soft collapse)	Post-liminality; "Anybody's game"; the "new public policy"
Old epistemic	Dominant	Fraying in the face of complex problems	Doubling-down through superficial advances (e.g., technology)
New epistemic	Unthinkable; impractical	Untested but plausible alternatives	Assertive; emergent

Indeed, scholars eschewing essentialist definitions of public policy, such as Freeman (2012), recognize the policy epistemic as fluid, evolving, and diverse; the challenge is to consider whether the collective script of a shared understanding of public policy (Freeman, 2012, p. 13) is itself a violation of non-essentialism or whether, for practical reasons and theoretical development, the field should undertake a course correction to prepare for epistemic liminality and what emerges thereafter.

Section 4 orients our theoretical argument into an actionable frame, examining how three ways of policy thinking – labeled technocratic, Frankfurt, and predicament – treat the issue of epistemic instability and the liminality of soft collapse in the context of policy change. We close with a discussion about the difficulties of activating an epistemic transition as against those of engaging in mere alteration to policy logics. We present a case for a paradigm shift in policy thinking, drawing on ideas about how revolutionary thought emerges in policy contexts. Our claim is that radical changes in the ossified and unsustainable epistemic logics of the world's economies, societies, politics, and cultures will probably fail to outpace the march of climate catastrophe and systemic collapse. The alternative, we propose, is an epistemic shift forced by the collapse itself, at cost to life, livelihood, and the ecosystem. From the collapse emerges a reboot of civilization and a re-starting of history. Under the old civilization, collapsing structures were the midwife of change because social systems are often fundamentally conservative, slow to change, and thus anachronistic. This, we argue, is no recipe for addressing emergent existential crises. The inability of society to transform itself in avoiding the catastrophic effects of such crises becomes the end of history. The midwife of change, however, lacks patience and proceeds with the collapse, rendering existing theories and institutions meaningless and thereby providing space for the emergence of a new ontology – a thing created by human agency in an era where no way of thinking is more epistemically privileged than the next. The "new public policy" emerges from this liminal state and is unknowable – a source both of its intrigue and also of its theoretical and empirical elusiveness. This Element attempts to prompt a scholarly reckoning with this challenge.

Our diagnosis, while seemingly pessimistic, establishes the foundation for a clean slate in how policy problems are understood – pointing towards a potentially fruitful new era of research and practice that considers the richness of diverse perspectives and opportunities to de-normalize and de-mainstream policy solutionism. Indeed, the ongoing collapse gives society an opportunity to free itself from structures and habits that valorize and privilege old thinking to make space for new. New structures emerging from collapse, no revolution but an organic process, also allow for a *carte blanche* phase of systemic reorganization and reconceptualization that bears the emergent property of new thinking. Such a process would unfold across arcs of time that go beyond most policy horizons and the three-, five-, and ten-year thinking bequeathed to the public policy field by practices in corporate strategy making. Even longer-term strategic horizons, such as the visions for mid-century transition adopted by global governance institutions, may be too short to allow the time needed for critical reflection, systemic reorganization, and a fundamental re-enlightenment to play out. As such, policy problems and their epistemics in a state of liminality raise numerous questions while answering few and thus deserve scholarly attention at this early stage of collapse. This Element provides no definitive resolutions but offers the basis for the twenty-first-century's existential call to action, one that should be heeded by the field of public policy even as the emperor's clothes fall to the ground.

2 The Convergence of Crises Leading to Soft Collapse

2.1 Convergent Crises in the Twenty-first Century

The convergence of environmental, social, and economic problems in the twenty-first century can be seen as a meta-crisis that tests not only the adaptability of society but also the definitional and analytical efforts of policy scholarship. We propose that society is in a state of ecological overshoot whose consequences interact with social, economic, and political forces to threaten wide-scale, hard collapse of human systems and institutions. A soft collapse, now in its initial measurable stages, had the potential to be accelerated by many types of systemic crises and indeed has been by the emergence of a pandemic that caught many by surprise. The explanations and narratives emerging from the crisis reveal rifts in how society interprets warning signs of its own demise. Some leaders and politicians refer to the pandemic as an aberrant inconvenience cynically exploited by their political rivals; scientists and many policy analysts, however, take a more sober view. It is evident, then, that the moment of pandemic-induced transition is seen more fully by some epistemic perspectives than by others. Additionally, it is lived more fully by some communities and groups than by others.

If we are to see COVID-19 as a catalyst for a collapse-driven systemic transition, the question about where the transition originated and where it may lead can be determined by how the pre-transition era was defined; commonly, it may be considered the "modern era." How, then, could an era characterized by sophisticated technology, governance systems, and empiricist ways of thinking and knowing – representing the seeming apex of human achievement to date – become so quickly and thoroughly destabilized? One answer is that the advancement and rationality of human systems was an illusion enabled by technological and technocratic "patching" of policy faults and by narratives that fortified the legitimacy of existing systems. Advancements in technology have enabled the further sophistication of policy tools, generating a race in which society was forced to continually outrun problems that it was itself creating through resource depletion, with market making and the commodification of production implicating the neoliberal globalization project. The systems of human mobility accompanying this process were also poised to create vectors of virus transmission. Indeed, the pre-globalization era and even premodern era experienced pandemics, but the rapid spread of COVID-19 was perceived as alarming and even unprecedented (Mas-Coma et al., 2020; Whitworth, 2020).

While society has faced numerous large-scale problems including world wars, civil wars, famines, pandemics, and injustices like colonization and widespread chattel slavery in the Western world, it is fair to consider how this crisis is different. The uniqueness is in its synchronicity. Some festering policy problems had not breached the threshold of urgency and visibility to earn political salience, due to the veneer of stability offered by patchwork solutions often drawing on technology. Those failed narratives were used to reframe problems as solvable, inevitable, or less urgent than they might appear. The backdrop for COVID-19 was a looming food crisis that had long outpaced the green revolution of the 1960s (Anthem, 2020) and domestic political and geopolitical tensions resulting from globalization-induced economic precarity (as manifest in the elections of populist and isolationist leaders; Rodrik, 2018). Adding further richness to the context of COVID-19 was the unabated environmental degradation and climate change resulting from humanity's voracious appetite for natural resources in service to the economic imperative of perpetual growth (Homer-Dixon, 2006). The global scientific community had already been warning of catastrophic effects resulting from climate change, including a broadly circulated report by the Intergovernmental Panel on Climate Change (IPCC) and the warning of a climate emergency issued by more than 11,000 scientists (Ripple et al., 2020). Arguably, any one of these problems exhibits wicked complexity,[2] but their confluence multiplied complexity to levels that human political, economic, and analytical systems were already struggling to fully comprehend and reconcile. Then came COVID-19.

According to Kuecker (2020), the pandemic precipitated an "abrupt loss of complexity." For the first extended period of time in modern history, systems of production and trade and flows of goods and people experienced an immediate

---

[2] There is an advanced literature on complexity theory that helps conceptualize the role of public policy (Geyer and Cairney, 2015; Freeman, 2012; Room, 2011; Byrne, 1998; Waldrop, 1992).

and jolting decline. Unemployment quickly spiked to levels not seen since the Great Depression. The policy reaction was decidedly Keynesian; many countries implemented massive unemployment and stimulus programs to the putative chagrin of the free-market apologists whose ideas had won the preceding decades. The effects of sudden economic retrenchment were also immediately apparent in the natural world, as pollution from factories and transportation sharply declined. The severity of this event was captured for a brief time during which the price of oil fell into the negative range (Cole, 2020). One of humanity's most precious commodities – fossil fuels – had by the prevailing economic rule set been rendered less than useless, momentarily illustrating how the economic system would react to a transformation in lifestyles or transition to new sources of energy.

COVID-19 was a catalyst for exposing existing frailties of the global system. These frailties had been long studied in their silos, but this historical moment brought them together to illustrate that strong ties among weak elements make no durable system. The realization that the interconnectedness of the global system is not necessarily a guarantee of its own durability is one change in thinking that this Element argues must be undertaken by the field of public policy. It proposes that a meta-view of complex problems also recognizes the complexity of their interactions and thus at its logical conclusion elevates the scale of problems to that of the entire human world. While such a claim may appear hyperbolic, there is no shame in reading this crisis for exactly what it is: an existential punch to the gut of humankind. Interpreted through complex systems theory, the pandemic has ushered society out of the "conservation" phase (in which technology and tools of modernity are applied to economizing and legitimizing an ossified rule set) and has propelled society into the "release" phase of collapse in which the complex becomes simple because systems cease to function how they normally did, if at all. From a practical point of view, factories gradually reopened and flights haltingly resumed; society was destined to declare victory over the virus and resume pre-pandemic habits assured of its ability to spend, research, and tweet its way out of crisis. This return to seeming normalcy may be an illusion, however, as the underlying frailties of the system endure despite the symptoms being momentarily addressed; it is akin to the alcoholic sobering up for church. Academia and society more broadly need to create space for new ways of thinking about the essence and role of public policy and about the relationship between human and natural systems. To deepen the context and argument for such a proposal, the next subsection investigates the twentieth century's most organized and ambitious effort to do just that – and how it ultimately failed.

2.2 Policy Response: Sustainability as a Narrative

Sustainability is arguably the salient policy issue of the modern era but also has an extended history and provides a useful case for exploring the applied implications of the epistemic transition later in this Element. The first global efforts to confront sustainability challenges emerged in the late twentieth century. The Bruntland Commission's (1987) report *Our Common Future* stated, "we are serving a notice – an urgent notice based on the latest and best scientific evidence – that the time has come to take the decisions needed to secure the resources to sustain this and coming generations" (p. 11). Five years later, the Rio Earth Summit was the first substantial multilateral gathering focused on sustainability issues including energy, natural resource depletion, and the by-products of industrial production. By the beginning of the new millennium, the US Democratic Party nominated a presidential candidate, Al Gore, who was among the earliest high-profile advocates of mainstreaming sustainability issues; his first book, *Earth in the Balance* (Gore, 1992), addressed the social, political, and economic interconnectedness of what was at the time an already evident environmental crisis. Gore was also the first presidential candidate to make climate change a core issue for policy debate. While much of the early sustainability discussion was based on scientific projections and associated warnings, changes in the severity of climate change effects were not yet evident to many lay observers and political support for deep and costly policy interventions remained tepid.

Two decades into the twenty-first century, the impacts of climate change are increasingly evident (e.g., in extreme weather patterns, glacier and ice cap melt, and sea-level rise), leading scientists and progressive policymakers to see a rapidly approaching inflection point in the survival of the human race. There is a scientific consensus that environmental degradation resulting from human activity threatens human well-being, livelihoods, and survival. The previously referenced IPCC report[3] states that "populations at disproportionately higher risk of adverse consequences with global warming of 1.5°C and beyond include disadvantaged and vulnerable populations, some indigenous peoples, and local communities dependent on agricultural or coastal livelihoods" (B.5.1). Amid growing evidence and increasingly urgent projections, governments have begun to heed calls from scientists, activists, and the general public for policy action on climate change. Efforts vary across countries and among global protocols, and comparative studies have accordingly gained popularity (Schmidt and Fleig, 2018; Aldy et al, 2017; Bernauer and Böhmelt, 2013; Aldy et al.,

---

[3] www.ipcc.ch/sr15/chapter/spm/

2003). A 2019 call to action endorsed by tens of thousands of scientists begins with the following opening statement:

> *Scientists have a moral obligation to clearly warn humanity of any cata-strophic threat and to "tell it like it is." On the basis of this obligation and the graphical indicators presented below, we declare, with more than 11,000 scientist signatories from around the world, clearly and unequivocally that planet Earth is facing a climate emergency."* Ripple et al. (2020, p. 1)

The urgency for climate action is scientifically clear, and some broad efforts have been undertaken to coordinate policy intervention. At the collective level, global organizations like the United Nations (UN) have been instrumental in drawing attention to how interdependencies among countries shape the climate action agenda.

Scientific clarity on environmental crisis has engendered some urgency among public agencies and nongovernmental organizations and interest from research institutes, consultancies, and corporations; this urgency and interest have led to pressure for policy intervention and coordination at the global level through the Sustainable Development Goals (SDGs). As the successor to the Millennium Development Goals (MDGs) (which focused primarily on poverty reduction through economic growth), the SDGs embrace a wider conceptual-ization of development that adds environmental sustainability to an existing agenda focused on social equity. Moreover, the thematic connection between the MDGs and SDGs is evident in the pursuit of poverty alleviation through economic growth – a strategy that has exacerbated local environmental degrad-ation from rapid industrialization as fed by market making, rising incomes, and hyper-consumption in wealthier countries. The immediate impacts of local environmental degradation, in addition to longer-term impacts of global climate change at the local scale, underscore how the sustainable development agenda impacts vulnerable communities in two negative ways: economic and environ-mental exploitation. Indeed, the effects of development efforts in the Global South reflect the same policy missteps and short-sighted thinking that led to similarly harmful environmental consequences in the rapidly industrializing Global North of the nineteenth and twentieth centuries.

The challenges of SDG implementation and coordination at the national and local levels provide justification for collective action in the context of a global commons. A governance system highly fragmented at the global level and across subnational jurisdictions is the setting in which policymakers are now undertaking the sprawling task of climate action. While addressing policy challenges at various scales generates creative interventions suited to particular contexts, a global architecture of enforcement and monitoring appears to have the collateral benefit of ensuring that actions of some jurisdictions are not undercut by the slack or contradictory actions of others. At the same time, efforts to institutionalize and globalize accountability for SDG implementation are contestable and even problematic in geopolitical, economic, and social ways – particularly as countries with rapidly growing economies lay claim to the "right to develop by polluting" that was enjoyed by the Global North throughout the nineteenth and twentieth centuries. Along with persistent national-level inequities in the distribution of resources to fight climate change, these geopolitical and other capacity-determining factors require nuanced and conditional perspectives in the comparison process.

The SDG project in its global scope and economic impact exhibits how elite interests are legitimized and institutionalized and how legacy policy epistemics are reproduced. The visions of sustainability, as articulated by the SDGs, are politically agreed and rendered coherent at the highest global institutional scale, expressed through targets and indicators and reinforced in yearly meetings and summits. Efforts to measure national-level progress are guided by the specificity of indicators (e.g., Indicator 11.5.2: "Direct disaster economic loss in relation to global GDP, including disaster damage to critical infrastructure and disruption of basic services"[4]). Operationalizing the ambiguous and politically defined concept of "sustainability" through an index of quantitative metrics facilitates the difficult task of cross-country comparison and within-country longitudinal monitoring; this empirical exercise also supports a ranking system that names and shames underperforming countries while obscuring context-based determinants of performance variation. The processes by which targets are pursued at the national level and below is shaped by place-specific dynamics that influence how problems are understood and experienced. Adding further complexity to national and local SDG efforts is the concurrent pressure to comply with and seek validation from sustainability narratives prevailing among global institutions and within epistemic communities of academics, think tanks, institutes, private corporations, consultancies, state and local governments, and others. As such, normative isomorphism evolves out of the promotion of agreed narratives and reifies a power-knowledge nexus[5] that functions like the proverbial military-industrial complex – reproducing and

---

[4] https://medium.com/sdgs-resources/sdg-11-indicators-5a613061b3dc

[5] We define the "power-knowledge nexus" as a sociopolitical community in which the producers of knowledge (e.g., global development institutions, think tanks, consultancies, academics, and other self-referential experts) operate in service to elite political and economic constituencies, supporting hegemonic narratives that marginalize challenges to system properties that protect powerful interests. The concept is similar to that of the "iron triangle" (Heclo, 1978) but introduces the element of knowledge creation that invites deeper reflection on the role of institutionalized expertise.

validating itself by maintaining stable epistemic hegemony and promoting legible, sweeping, and rationally plausible (or commonsense) understandings about the definition and practice of sustainability. Through their self-referential expertise, nexus actors maintain elite position in society while giving perverse effect to the democratic elements of what policy science as a scholarly field labels the "intelligence function" (McDougal et al., 1973).

The SDG effort, like many other global protocols and reform movements for issues like corruption, human rights, and free trade, is perhaps the most complete example of how a coherent global vision is refracted through kaleidoscopes of national-level characteristics. As an historically unprecedented geopolitical policy exercise, the SDGs embody a veneer of collective agreement on problem definition while leaving the task of interpretation and monitoring largely to individual countries – a quasi-global-federalist model thin on accountability but laden with soft diplomatic coercion. The intelligence function, as discussed in Section 3 of this Element, is useful for understanding these dynamics, as it reflects the normalizing power (Foucault, 1988; Arendt, 1958) by which a particular agenda for understanding sustainability overlays scientific fact with social, economic, and political value framings. These framings are promoted by global knowledge and power elites, becoming received wisdom across society; a common example is the promotion of the market mechanism as a pathway toward emissions reduction through carbon credit-trading schemes. The intelligence function thus promotes a value-laden norm that members of the global community are assumed to embrace as common sense. This exercise in epistemic hegemony disciplines all related work – including narrative framing – by coercively normalizing how actors operate and think. Evidence is selected or interpreted to support the narrative consistency of preconceived problem framings that fit existing market solutions and are validated in reports by government agencies, NGOs, academics, development banks, the UN, and others. This dynamic prevents counter-hegemonic narratives (e.g., that the market mechanism is a cause of, rather than solution to, the sustainability problem) from becoming visible and credible, thereby limiting opportunities for paradigm shifts. As such, the need for deeper reflection within the policy field is evident – a matter explored in the following subsection.

2.3 Policy's Time of Reckoning

Within the span of eight months in late 2018 and early 2019, the UN released two reports whose scientific evidence suggests a time of reckoning for policy and humanity itself. The first, the IPCC Special Report on Global Warming of 1.5°C, warned in stark terms that deep and rapid reductions in carbon emissions are needed to prevent eventual climate catastrophe. The second, issued by the UN's Intergovernmental Science-Policy Platform on Biodiversity and Ecosystem Services (IPBES), provided a landmark assessment of the planetary ecosystem and warned of its collapse. Both reports are reminders of what Shiva stated in her 2010 Sydney Peace Prize acceptance speech: "When we think of wars in our times, our minds turn to Iraq and Afghanistan. But the bigger war is the war against the planet. This war has its roots in an economy that fails to respect ecological and ethical limits – limits to inequality, limits to injustice, limits to greed and economic concentration." Shiva's analysis echoed the words of Price (1990), who stated that "a new political and economic order may be emerging, as post-war ideological divisions start to break down … and questions of intergenerational equity begin to be taken into account in investment and resource management decisions" (p. 3). Threats to systemic stability and human survival are ubiquitous, interconnected, synchronous, and increasingly urgent. Systems theory scholarship (Homer-Dixon, 2006; Kuecker, 2007; Meadows et al., 2004) shows that the prospect of a perfect storm of crises is widely known among experts, but the translation of that knowledge into policy narratives and practice is problematic.

We turn in this subsection to a discussion about why and how certain sustainability policy approaches are unsuitable for twenty-first century problems characterized by unmanageable complexity. In so doing, we consider how the convergence of systemic crises destabilizes the practice of policymaking, and how an epistemic transition within policy could plausibly redefine how society conceptualizes itself, its relationship with the natural world, and its governing institutions and practices. While current policy practice influences society's early-stage interactions with the ecosystem's soft collapse, that influence is becoming weaker and less certain as evidence of its ineffectiveness accumulates. Anticipating the fate of policy as it faces these challenges, we ponder the extent to which policy's epistemic is fatally flawed in the face of the sustainability crisis and whether it can reconcile itself with wicked problems.

Two theoretical implications emerge from this line of inquiry. First, arguments about the gathering ineffectiveness of public policy invite consideration about what happens to knowledge while a system that gives knowledge credible effect is destabilized by collapse and undergoes transition. At the moment when a complex system tips into collapse or transitions into a new system, established knowledge structures – once deeply nested and long enjoying hegemonic influence – are disrupted and challenged. This process intensifies when a convergence of complex problems exposes the inability of old knowledge structures to understand, explain, or manage crises. At the climax of this process lies a tipping-point characterized by what Taylor (2001) calls the "moment of

complexity." The claims of destabilized knowledge mirror the system's oscillation between moments of collapse, transition, and reproduction, during which
once-established and credible wisdom scrambles to safeguard its authority amid
a swell of anomalous data (see Kuhn's (2012 [1962]) explanation of paradigm
shifts). During the moment of complexity, existing knowledge becomes anachronistic while new knowledge has yet to emerge. The result is a disorientating
"time of the posts" (Kuecker, 2004; Best and Kellner 1997) – a liminal state
between two moments: one past and one future. In this liminal state, knowledge
loses credibility and its power to explain and self-validate weakens. The
consequent loss of legitimacy triggers panic, defensiveness, resignation, or
other context-dependent behaviors among hegemonic interests that are supported by old knowledge and creates a vacuum for the emergence of alternative
knowledges. New systems of thought compete more evenly with the vestiges of
modernity's truth claims and legacy knowledge, with evident ramifications for
politics and policy.

Second, the argument about the gathering ineffectiveness of modern policy
implies the need for a hard reckoning about epistemic instability, especially
regarding potentially unresolvable tensions within legacy knowledge structures
(see Tyfield [2012] for a discussion about academic and policy-analytical
research amid disruption and global crises). Foremost, such a reckoning
would target the core of policy's power-knowledge nexus, its commonsense
apparatus constructed to address wicked problems in politically and economically acceptable ways, and the processes of validation and socialization within
knowledge communities (Hessels et al., 2019). A fruitful reckoning would
begin with experts who produce knowledge that informs policy (see
Grundmann [2017] for a discussion). Elite cadres of academics, consultants,
knowledge institutions, and public and private researchers act in self-interest by
generating politically legitimate policy ideas while defining the meaning of
expertise and authority in a way that fortifies their own legitimacy. The power to
influence not merely the policy outputs but also the architecture of the system
used to produce them protects the privileged stead of policy expertise from
indictments by paradigm-shifting anomalous data. Furthermore, the shared
system of thought, rooted in instrumental rationalism, leads elite cadres to see
all problems as empirically reducible, definable, and solvable. Despite this
performative legitimacy, technocratic rationalism is patently bewildered by
wicked problems, as evident in the failings of several of the twentieth century's
major policy projects; this suggests that such problems may more realistically
be seen as predicaments to be managed rather than solved. We argue that the
power-knowledge nexus formed around or in service to the discourse of the
Post-2015 Development Agenda, as described in the previous subsection,

legitimizes the same normative vision that has driven the global system to the brink of collapse.

In coping with the instabilities of the liminal state, it is necessary to locate policy practice and theory within the potential futures of systemic transition and what emerges thereafter. Confronting the transition problem mandates consideration of big questions in historical sociology, especially how macrostructural transformations materialize and, once in play, what their life cycles and processes of replication are. Addressing the issue of transition in ecological systems, Holling (1986) offers a heuristic in the four-phase cycle of adaptation – a closed infinity loop in which society proceeds recursively through exploitation, conservation, release, and reorganization. Scholars have variously applied the adaptive cycle concept to policy perspectives in studies about resilience (Duit, 2016; Steelman, 2016; Westley et al., 2013; Walker and Salt, 2006). We argue that efforts to understand the current period of reckoning and liminality benefit from theory-based explanations of change with particular reference to macro-systemic transitions in humanity's relationship with the environment as determined by social, political, and economic subsystems and peculiarities across countries and societies. The relationship of the soft collapse hypothesis to policy sciences is that policy as a scholarly field professes to explain and establish the processes by which societal problems are understood and as a practical field professes to frame, institutionalize, and actualize possible solutions. Under a soft collapse scenario,[6] however, contexts radically change and thus render anachronistic the received scholarly and practical understandings of public policy.

Section 2 offered an overview of this Element's case for a new policy epistemic. The subsequent theoretical discussion is used to further understand the sustainability crisis and to argue that society has passed an inflection point beyond which public policy will not look or function as it did in the modern era.

---

[6] We propose that there are four possible transition scenarios. First, human systems can persist in their current state of unsustainable growth and ecological overshoot, with dire consequences. Second, human systems can undergo a catastrophic collapse (the longer-term eventuality of the first path) with the legacy epistemic tenuously maintaining only artificially constructed legitimacy or losing it altogether. Third, human systems can experience a soft collapse with staged losses of complexity over time, mitigating impacts as they arise and leveraging opportunities for longer-term innovation and renewal. Finally, human systems can experience a transition from one state to another without a collapse, the unlikeliest scenario as systemic change rarely occurs without a catastrophic impetus. Policy's wicked problem challenge is that any of these four scenarios is plausible, particularly at early stages of transition. It is thus incumbent on policy scholars to reflect on multiple scenarios, including these and possibly others, that dictate the shifting context of policy practice; according to Peters (2017), "given the link of wicked problems to complexity theory it would be useful to consider some of the premises of that approach in any research program. For example, although perhaps implied in the discussion of wicked problems the notions of non-linearity and multifinality that abide in complexity" (p. 394).

We selected sustainability and climate change as the underlying theme but sought to connect these challenges with others through the notions of wicked problems and problem convergence; the proposition is that the existing rifts, frailties, and failures of society have been rhetorically or technocratically patched well enough to obscure the profound severity of systemic problems. Overlaying novel crises onto systemic problems exposes the folly of patchwork solutionism. The consequent soft collapse, one in which society clings to old epistemics, narratives, and institutions even as their shortcomings are exposed, is humanity's new context – one that diverges from the old context around which the policy field developed and ossified its ways of thinking and doing. The new context emerging from the liminal state of transition is unknowable, but scholars can anticipate and prepare for it by critically interrogating the epistemic roots of the policy field itself with an eye toward new theoretical space.

Section 3 proceeds by examining the evolution of theories that constitute the legacy of the modern policy epistemic. It begins with an examination of instrumental rationalism and the ongoing reign of quantification in policy research. The policy sciences as a field are then explored as a response to rigid empiricism that seeks to account for context and embraces values and politics as fundamental elements of a pragmatic view on policy reality. We conclude Section 3 by examining the increasing visibility of alternative narratives as challenges to hegemonic policy narratives, and by discussing the prospect of "other knowledges" to assert their perspectives in the policy process.

Section 4 then proceeds with two subsections. The first explores the intersections of epistemic instability and practical dimensions of the transition problem by examining wicked problems as a set of intractable challenges threatening to undermine policy's hegemonic status and credibility. We place these challenges within three modes of thinking: technocratic, Frankfurt, and predicament. The first and second represent, respectively, practical and theoretical perspectives about the definition of problems and the epistemic foundations of related analysis; the third considers technology-informed thinking more broadly and futures such as AI and machine learning more narrowly as emerging but uncertain forces driving transition. The second and final subsection of Section 4 brings into sharper focus the transition problem by applying at a macro level three of the most commonly cited frameworks of policy transition and change: multiple streams, advocacy coalition, and punctuated equilibrium.[7]

---

[7] As we later do for multiple streams and advocacy coalition frameworks, we use the term "framework" in reference to the concept of "punctuated equilibrium," acknowledging that unlike the other two it is typically referenced as a theory. We contend that this semantic shortcut is not

Each is overlaid with the proposed three modes of thinking in an analysis that considers the actions of individuals, collectives, and the institutions that delimit them. The final exercise serves the Element's purpose to demonstrate how a new epistemic approach does not need to wholly depart from decades of literature on public policy but can in its novelty compel scholars to revisit foundational ideas, identify unexploited space for theoretical development within them, and apply them in novel ways to ideas about public policy that better align with the increasingly observable realities of systemic collapse.

3 Theoretical Evolution from Instrumental Rationalism to Policy Sciences

3.1 The Sad History of Instrumental Rationalism

While governments toil with the mechanics of policy coordination and implementation, myriad ecological, social, and economic problems invite a critical-epistemic reflection. This critical perspective can offer an alternative explanation for why decades of research in political and social sciences have not provided full understandings about the nature and stubbornness of complex problems like the climate crisis. The inability of public policy to respond well to complex problems has been variously explained across the literature, including policy failure (Mukhtarov and Gerlak, 2014; Howlett, 2012; McConnell, 2010; Tenbensel, 2006), institutionalisms of various sorts (historical, rational choice, and sociological; Hall and Taylor, 1996), deficiencies in policy instrument matching (Howlett, 2018), and politics (Dryzek, 1990), among others. We argue that policy's often faulty and deficient response to complex problems can be traced to the Western Enlightenment's (hereafter, "Enlightenment") valorization of scientific logic as an unassailable form of intellectual reasoning, and to the later application of scientific positivism to social questions (for an overview and critique of positivism and logical empiricism, see Caldwell, 2015).[8] Enlightenment rationalism, which four centuries ago embarked on an effort to transform existing ways of knowing and being at the individual and collective levels, precipitated an epistemic turn away from spiritual and religious

---

detrimental to the validity of our argument. For a discussion about the distinctions among models, theories, and frameworks, see Ostrom (2011).

[8] We acknowledge the normative dilemma of ascribing counterproductive elements of policy thinking to ideas extending from the Enlightenment (Oreskes and Conway, 2013). Objectively positive ideas and institutions – and variants interpreted as society progressed – emerged from the Enlightenment, including humanism, universal rights, notions of "freedom," better medicine, and better working and living conditions for workers. At the same time, it is fair to trace the origins of modern epistemics – at their best and worst – to the Enlightenment, as the claim supports our argument about how policy thinking has ossified through the processes of epistemic path dependency and socio-political embeddedness.

explanations of reality and toward formal scientific measurement and objectivity (Arato et al., 1978). Rationalism's allure was based, among other things, on the objectivity of systematic observation and intellectual reasoning as against subjective, divine, or mystical reflection. The social, political, and economic ramifications were substantial and enduring; undermining the credibility of sacred and influential institutions like the Catholic Church threatened to destabilize social hierarchies, the "divine" rights of political leadership, and economic interests protected by both. Notably, communities and "traditional" societies around the world had long embraced what Western modernity would later recognize as science and rationalism, evident in the engineering feats of complex structures and cities of the ancient world; even from a social scientific perspective, the ancient world was home to vast civilizations and multi-faceted bureaucracies. Nevertheless, the Enlightenment iteration of rationalist thinking stridently bore the emblem of epistemic modernization and profoundly impacted modern social sciences in ways that endure to this day.

The broad scope of the Enlightenment provided a foundation for the application of epistemic rationalism to all aspects of the human experience, extending originally from natural science to social science and ultimately to the logic of how society organizes itself economically and politically. This totalizing exercise in societal modernization and rationalism never reached its full apotheosis but appeared to climax with the development of positivist perspectives and the enabling methods (e.g., technology) that attempted to metricize social phenomena and facilitate application of the scientific method to questions about individual and collective human behavior. Positivism came into vogue toward the end of the nineteenth century by challenging existing scholarly understandings about social sciences; through Taylorism (Taylor, 1911), it ultimately shaped the practice of organization management both public and private. With the "rule of reason" generating its own creed, Enlightenment rationalism posited that society works best when the individual pursues his or her rational self-interest, and that the aggregation of these rational behaviors across a society would lead to the optimal allocation of effort and resources; the familiar tenets of classical economic theory (e.g., Adam Smith's "invisible hand") are one expression of this ideal. By the mid-twentieth century, rationalist policy methods were confronted with the uncomfortable realities of wicked social problems too disruptive to politically ignore (e.g., poverty and discrimination). Instrumental rationalism, however, failed the test of epistemic disruption while public policy plodded forward with incomplete and unsustainable 'solutions" that, in many cases, further exacerbated problems. Policy scholarship theorized this somewhat adaptive policymaking method as incrementalism or, more colloquially, "muddling through" (Lindblom, 1979). It is plausible that the convergence of deepening rationalism and the rise of social problems was no coincidence at all – the disruption emerged as a consequence of policy's reliance on the rationalist instruments of Enlightenment thinking (see Scott, 1998). At this stage of our argument, we acknowledge the rich, creative, and often helpful literature that takes varying critical perspectives on the study and practice of public policy (see Fischer et al. [2015] for an overview). Indeed, there are multiple understandings about complex phenomena and wicked problems, including but not limited to those previously listed. Many have influenced the practice of policy in material ways, with many governments – even if in halting ways – acknowledging the intractability of policy problems and the need to think differently about how to address them. Nevertheless, positivism and its practical manifestation through instrumental rationalism became and remains the dominant trajectory and is thus the prime subject of this Element's critique.

The dilemma of instrumental rationalism is not necessarily its mismatch with all policy problems but with increasingly complex ones. Many policy problems have clear and largely uncontested definitions, simplifying – from a political perspective – the application of technologies within ring-fenced or well-defined contexts. For example, traffic congestion can be addressed not only through street redesign but also through the application of smart systems that monitor conditions and suggest alternative routes to drivers. Legitimate success in the ring-fenced application of instrumental rationalism to well-defined problems, however, has engendered what we argue is an illusory faith in the ability of instrumental rationalism to address all types of problems – particularly as definitions and determinants have become more complex and contested. Furthermore, even the seemingly successful application of instrumental rationalism to well-defined problems produced effects that later became wicked problems. For example, to extend the traffic illustration, greater efficiency in suggested routing for automobiles and optimization of commercial routes distribute congestion and its effects at a wider geographic scale and at some cost to uncompensated parties; it does not, however, address the underlying structural determinants of increasing congestion, including car-centric urban design and societal nudges toward car ownership over transit use. The same dynamic can be said to exist when observing any sort of individually rational but collectively suboptimal behavior, including activities that degrade the environment and cause climate change. These tools win the moment but fail in the longer run, providing only the veneer of success and serving whatever political or commercial imperative prevails at the time. They also fail to recognize the complexity, uncertainty, and interconnectivity that increasingly characterize the convergence of wicked policy problems. As implied by Hitch (1957) in the following quote, common policy-analytic tools have been helpful only when applied to certain types of problems; indeed, their success with such problems may engender greater (but ultimately misplaced) faith in the ability of such tools to help policymakers understand more complex problems:

> *The sort of simple explicit model which operations researchers are so profi-*
> *cient in using can certainly reflect most of the significant factors influencing*
> *traffic control on the George Washington Bridge, but the proportion of the*
> *relevant reality which we can represent by any such model or models in*
> *studying, say, a major foreign-policy decision, appears to be almost trivial.*
> (Hitch, 1957, p. 718).

Quick-win solutions offered by the tools of instrumental rationalism can thus conceal faults in underlying systems, as policy models drawing on Enlightenment self-interest incentivize behavior that is individually rational but collectively detrimental. Even where such systems fail, their political, economic, and technological advocates excuse their faults by insisting on the need for only minor tweaking and re-calibration or simply more time to produce benefits; this cycle illustrates how policy doubles-down on legacy thinking and exacerbates problems by doing the wrong things more quickly and efficiently based on the narrow set of performance metrics often adopted. Failure is explained not by a mismatch between policy problems and the conceptual underpinnings of policy tools but by bad implementation, political impatience, insufficient resource commitment, or unfortunate aberrance. Through repeated instances of this way of thinking, the rationalist epistemic has evolved via an institutional path dependency to become the dominant rule set for how global economic, social, and political systems work. As such, deviation from the system becomes infeasible due to a lack of opportunities to generate a critical mass of anomalous data (see Kuhn's (2012 [1962]) concept of "scientific revolution"); this stasis perpetuates the hegemony of the epistemic. Instrumental rationalism has become not only a rule set but a basis for common sense itself, reproducing to the extent that a particular way of thinking and being feels so natural and organic that it fails to prompt reflection or pushback. This hegemonizing appears to reflect the justifiably inevitable victory of good ideas and thus has substantial logical appeal, but upon more critical reflection, it is a product of institutional structures that proactively limit and enable the limita-tion of epistemic frames, thereby shaping policy thinking in predetermined ways. Policymakers often inherit and re-perform this ossified script without any meta-cognition (e.g., "now I will apply this epistemic") or critical reflection (e.g., "is this an appropriate problem frame?"). Understandings by policy-makers about policy problems are either predetermined and handed down through institutional legacy or obtained from common and embedded ways of managing and interpreting information (i.e., those learned in policy schools that have been normalized to global practice through accreditation). Whether the tool-problem mismatch is a result of willful denial or of hapless adaptation by policymakers to evolving conditions, challenges to the prevailing epistemic of instrumental rationalism are often met in political and academic circles with a skepticism borne of ideological territorialism and protectionism.

The aspirational exercise of problem solving itself – connecting a clearly defined problem with a correspondingly targeted policy tool – is a common trap ensnaring the instrumental-rationalist epistemic. Enabling assumptions are based on an incomplete account of confounding variables (i.e., only those that can be measured), leading to a policy prescription so laden with qualifications and contextual caveats that it holds value only as a general or even nebulous ideal. The fallacy of this approach as applied to the social sciences is clear; context can rarely be fully empiricized and thus eludes the gaze of many popular empirical models. This describes the problem-solving epistemic implied in Lasswell's concepts of problem orientation (1970) and problem attitude (1951) and contrasts with what we later describe as "predicament thinking" in which policy prescriptions recognize their limitations and seek not to solve problems but to manage the impacts of unsolvable crises (Hartley et al., 2019). As such, a methodological bias has shaped ideas that dominate not only the practice but also the study of public policy. Indeed, policy practice has exhibited little meaningful self-reflection in acknowledging its own entrenched problem-solving epistemic, while academia appears marginally more critical but its tone is generally revisionist rather than revolutionary; one must visit the far reaches of the literature to find calls for transformation requiring more than mere tinkering and window dressing.

While this Element has referred to the social sciences as a monolithic construct, a robust interrogation of policy epistemics implies the need to recognize some differences among social science disciplines. For example, economics has a deep legacy of epistemic rationalism, owing in large part to its quantitative foundations. The rational-scientific hierarchy of the social sciences in modern academe, however artificially constructed and unfairly imposed, is evident to most who work within them; economics occupies one stratum and the rest (e.g., sociology, political science, and anthropology) an empirically subordinate one. Within the field of public policy and administration, a rationalist-epistemic orthodoxy appears to monopolize mainstream scholarship, and with the complicity of managerialist tenure review practices has led to the rigid quantification of publication output as the primary indicator of research productivity (Lynch, 2015). Such practices incentivize output quantity and thus privilege the type of empirical approaches popular among economists; notably, this reveals a connection between epistemic rationalism in the content of scholarly work and the same in systems to evaluate that work. Although the policy literature appears still to cleave into positivist and interpretivist camps, the former is arguably predominant – particularly among research grant-making bodies. The positivist camp has a long tradition in public administration, borne of Taylorism and surviving in managerialist paradigms such as new public management (Pollitt, 2007). While these paradigms may assume differing narratives in accordance with evolving problem contexts (e.g., climate change), the methods of practicing them – and of measuring and studying them – remain embedded in rationalist models based on inputs, outputs, problems, and solutions. The policy literature, in its efforts to rationalize the complex and often chaotic endeavor of policymaking within shifting contexts, likewise succumbed in large measure to this epistemic bias; examples are the conceptualization of a seemingly ordered and sequential process of policy stages and the navel-gazing focus on technocratic elements of policymaking such as policy instruments, tools, settings, and capacities. The logic is that the proper calibration and combination of these elements lead to quantitatively and qualitatively optimal solutions. While the epistemics of such approaches are applicable to certain types of problems, they lose currency in addressing more complex problems because they fail to see what is unmeasurable but still consequential.

To connect this line of argument to the Element's broader theme, we maintain that the benefits of applying instrumental rationalism as a didactic and analytical philosophy are nearing or have reached their exhaustion, particularly with reference to complex problems; this is the source of what we consider to be the field's increasingly anachronistic nature. The frontiers of policy literature continue, at this moment, to be a rather technocratic interest in instruments and capacities. This interest dovetails conveniently with advances in technology as a means to measure and analyze. At the same time, concepts like "actors," "ideas," and "institutions" enjoy a rich literature and, particularly during an era of populism and contestation of fact, fruitful opportunities to reconnect policy and politics in scholarship. As much as the practice of policy has seen limited success in providing guidance that is useful and appropriate for navigating complexity, so too does the policy literature appear to be struggling to explain this failure. Instead of advocating that the field plod forward with incremental amendments to current theories and practices, this Element proceeds in the next section to identify the faults of some long-held theoretical tenets, to mine fresh insights where possible in foundational concepts of the policy sciences, and to explore how those insights might be dissociated with anachronistic thinking to provide the seeds of new thinking or complement emergent epistemics. This search for latent wisdom can illuminate new perspectives on wicked problems such as the climate crisis and can be applicable during the coming period of epistemic liminality and post-liminal epistemic emergence. More specifically, the following section examines Lasswell's intelligence function and the perspective of policy sciences on the nexus between political power and scientific knowledge, heeding this Element's call for a renewed connection between policy and politics as a means to understand and address systemic collapse. These ideas are selected because, in practice, they are shaped by the dominant epistemic orientation of policymaking as previously outlined, whether pure instrumental-rationalist or some variant.

3.2 Policy Sciences: Getting Intellectual about Intelligence

Lasswell (1970) described the policy sciences as "knowledge of the policy process and of the relevance of knowledge in the policy process" (p. 3). Of particular relevance to this Element's argument about epistemic transition are Lasswell's view of knowledge as constructed and contested, an idea developed later in his career and arguably ahead of its time. An underexplored implication of Lasswell's view is that the policy sciences can provide useful insights into the forces behind epistemic lock-in and the marginalization of alternative knowledges and narratives as they relate to problem framing. This section draws on the seminal ideas of Lasswell, McDougal, and others having deep familiarity with Lasswell's work and the man himself, including Dunn, Farr, and Ascher. The purpose is to capture the foundational tenets of the policy sciences independent of efforts to refashion them into the rationalist epistemic logic we critique in this Element or to unduly attribute to Lasswell credit or blame for valorizing technocracy as it existed in his time or thereafter. In particular, this section explores ideas about the intelligence function and participation among expert and nonexpert parties in the largely technocratic practice of policymaking. The purpose of the discussion is to understand how scholars have understood policy knowledge and its development and incorporation into the policymaking process; we argue that that policy knowledge and the intelligence function are crucial determinants of the field's epistemic orientation and thus impact how problems are constructed.

According to McDougal et al. (1972), intelligence as it relates to policy "involves the acquisition of information and planning in exercise of all five of the intellectual tasks required of decisionmakers" (p. 365). Lasswell (1970) outlines these tasks as goal clarification; trend description; analysis of conditions; projection of future developments; and invention, evaluation, and selection of alternatives. These are nested within the larger policy process framework, of which the constitutive elements are agenda setting, policy options formulation, decision-making, implementation, and evaluation (in no particular order, as they can occur at the same time). Lasswell's 1951 chapter "The Policy Orientation" provides insights into his formative ideas about the intelligence function as a crucial element of the policy process and by extension effective policymaking: "if the rationality of the policy process is to be improved, we must single out the intelligence function for special study" (p. 4). Lasswell's explicit connection between intelligence and rationality became a foundational tenet for technocratic policymaking and what critics described as an elitist process, even if Lasswell did not explicitly present it as such. Through his ideas about the "policy scientist of democracy," Lasswell articulated a construct of rationality based on the use of scientific evidence by professional policymakers in the identification of problems and prescription of solutions with a normative orientation towards the common good (Kay, 2011). According to this logic, the means to prevent malicious capture of policymaking were democratic checks and balances and the goodwill of an enlightened elite. The normative political qualities of the intelligence function, such as they could be identified in practice, were embodied in Lasswell's call for the intelligence function to consider context (a fundamental tenet of the policy sciences framework) – leaving open the potential for alternative epistemics to emerge but not calling explicitly for anti-rationalist pushback. As the concept of the policy scientist of democracy was not fully elaborated by Lasswell himself, its ambiguities have allowed various understandings to emerge. We read in Lasswell's work some pathways not only for how to "rescue" his legacy from the clutches of instrumental-rationalist expropriation but also for how the dominant policy epistemic can begin to be disassembled and re-thought amid the notion of shifting context that Lasswell emphasized.

Lasswell's vision of rationality had roots in the philosophical pragmatist movement exemplified by the work of John Dewey and others advocating practical efficacy as against top-down intervention based on Cartesian objectivity (see Dewey [1931] and Kaufman-Osborn [1985] for background about the evolution of these and related ideas). Scholars used Lasswell's logic to justify sweeping technocratic policy interventions and instrumental rectitude. Underpinning pragmatist policy logic is the idea that credibility and verification extend from collective agreement within a society; this is an illustration of how the policy sciences are themselves socially embedded and the act of policymaking fundamentally political even if concurrently technocratic. These dynamics are reflected in the membership profile of empowered subgroups (e.g., the scientific and political elite versus the general public) and in the degree of influence non-elite society has on policymaking. Given the tensions evident in policy sciences and other social sciences, Dewey (1931) contemplated the boundaries between political practice and knowledge, from which a direct line can be drawn to Lasswell's concept of the policy scientist of democracy as an aspirational model of a technically capable and socially enlightened public servant pursuing the collective good. Indeed, Dewey recognized the value of understanding society as the aggregation of individuals" interests, biases, and cognitive functions: "pragmatism and instrumental experimentalism bring into prominence the importance of the individual. It is he who is the carrier of creative thought, the author of action, and of its application" (in Hickman and Alexander, 1998, p. 12). A whiff of Enlightenment individualism can be detected in such thinking – ostensibly mute on ideology while speaking to how policies change and societies evolve. The narrative of the "benevolent technocrat" endures to this day – a useful rhetorical device to reconcile the increasingly technologically informed management of society with calls for more inclusive and participatory governance. In this seemingly commonsense approach to reconciling expert management with political realities, defenders of legacy thinking find a strong case for validation and a superficially convincing answer to accusations of policy capture and technocratic fundamentalism.

Closer examination of how scholars and practitioners have interpreted and reshaped these foundational ideas over time, in ways that constitute what is now understood as the policy sciences, reveals some conceptual misalignment with the nature of modern policy challenges. One way to understand this potential misalignment is by examining how policy problems are defined. According to Farr et al. (2008): "perhaps the most valuable and easily transferable contribution of the policy sciences is the demand that the social sciences be 'problem oriented'" (p. 30). As argued in the preceding section, the ossified problem-solving epistemic of modern policy practice is the apotheosis of instrumental rationalism. The epistemic's liabilities as an ineffective and potentially counterproductive way of understanding problems lies in the essentialist claim that problem definitions are clear, scientifically defensible, and politically uncontested. Although most policy perspectives (including technocratic ones) recognize context and complexity, efforts to modernize or advance policy practice focus still on bringing better definitional clarity to problem understandings (whether through technology, improved policy practice, or democratization and participation); depending on how such efforts proceed, this approach risks narrowly defining what policy sees based only on the tools of observation and analysis at hand. These approaches are deeply rooted in legacy thinking, with the formative policy sciences literature providing examples of how complex issues can be better confronted amid uncertainty. For example, McDougal et al. (1973) argued that rationalism is "an interaction between explicit or implicit goals and a constant flow of information about the environment"

(p. 366). Rationalism does not deny the presence of complexity but for analytical or political purposes seeks to tame it. McDougal's explicit or implicit goals would reflect in discussions of sustainability a set of policy visions collectively agreed upon by climate scientists and policymakers and more broadly under the model of collaborative internationalism facilitated by multilateral institutions like the United Nations. Of greater intrigue in McDougal's statement is the dynamism of evolving (and measurable) circumstances, reminiscent of the fluidity characterizing wicked problems like climate change. Data generated by information-gathering systems designed around a particular epistemic vary over time and would appear to provide updated understandings about problems; nevertheless, these systems are epistemically incapable of recognizing the type of anomalous data that would challenge not only the outputs of existing policy thinking but also the logic behind how that thinking occurs. A crucial point, then, is that this phenomenon does not invalidate McDougal's argument but illustrates how the argument applies to a shifting context in which the constant flow of information is more broadly encompassing and thus better reflective of reality. It is how the information is treated, understood, and incorporated into policy change that presents a lingering intrigue concerning the perpetuation of technocratic and instrumental-rationalist thinking in the policy field. In this way, the Lasswellian tradition provides the conceptual building blocks, but the foundation supporting those building blocks, and the institutional structure they constitute, is being destabilized by shifting contexts – this is the source of the field's anachronism. Our argument is not that Lasswell has failed to think of everything, but that understandings and practices built on this intellectual legacy have become so ossified that they prevent productive critical reassessment of their own foundational epistemic concepts.

To view this epistemic at work, one may turn no further than to how policy problems are understood. Naming and framing policy problems are fraught undertakings, as information can be challenged in political settings (Fischer, 2019; Fisher et al., 2012; Dunlap and McCright, 2011). This is particularly evident in the ongoing debates in the United States about the causes of climate change and policy interventions to address them. According to Ascher (2007), "the analytic exercise of problem definition is a combination of establishing what values are at stake and mapping out potential diagnoses of the roots of the problem. Therefore, problem definition is both a normative and analytical effort" (p. 142). Political power in this case can be described as the ability or privilege of defining the normative frame shaping narratives about policy problems – a principal source of legitimacy within the power-knowledge nexus. With the privilege of problem definition (e.g., naming climate change as a threat to capitalist economic interests) comes influence over the design and execution of research and over information feedback loops constructed within particular normative frames. In this way, the intelligence function can become an impenetrable fortress of ideology in which narratives reproduce themselves, neutralizing the potentially beneficial effects of information flow (particularly amid shifting contexts). The wicked nature of modern policy problems like climate change implies that the definition of problems is no simple task; however, within the power-knowledge nexus, the complexity of defining problems is less about the characteristics of problems themselves (e.g., their complexity, interconnectedness, urgency, and uncertainty) than about internal processes, negotiations, and struggles among elite interests over how the terms of information gathering and analysis are established, validated, and revised. We argue that this logic of practice, as theoretically illustrated (or exposed) by policy sciences and the intelligence function, implicates itself in exacerbating the very problems it claims to solve. The corollary argument is that liberal internationalism is normatively oriented in that it seeks to make global systems stable for and receptive to capitalist expansion. The sustainability discourse itself is reformist beyond ecological matters, particularly in its coercive promotion of market mechanisms and technology that passes for common sense but leads ultimately to further capitalist reproduction. Epistemic lock-in, valorized through the (mis)use of knowledge management properties illustrated in Lasswell's intelligence function, yields a stable policy agenda whose occasional variations in framing give the appearance of substantive reform while fortifying system properties against threats (including climate change) to the economic and political status quo. When applications and incarnations of the intelligence function are seen from this critical perspective, they present themselves as a deceptive form of hegemony in which the power-knowledge nexus cycle functionally if not intentionally conceals a deeper agenda of reproduction rather than transformation. In this way, public policy's dominant way of thinking is incapable of self-liberation and thus becomes anachronistic as contextual circumstances shift.

The technocratic gestures of instrumental rationalism, even if insulated from political contestation and power games, would still struggle to cope with wicked problems because contextual factors that cannot be measured and harmonized with existing data and narrative frames are simplified as controls if not treated as entirely extraneous in modeling exercises. The models themselves are conceived with the endorsement of the power-knowledge nexus, by experts socialized or professionalized to serve vested interests and credentialed by institutions beholden to powerful interests in various ways. This nexus actively limits the field of policy possibilities by making some things visible and others invisible through social-scientistic reductionism. For example, in measuring gross domestic product (GDP), only certain aspects of the economy are made visible (e.g., production) while others are made invisible (e.g., the social effects of environmental degradation); the effect in this example is that benefits are unduly weighted in relation to costs. The narratives of instrumental rationalism express little self-reflection about such flaws and instead assume an empiricist hubris that substantiates their monopolization of universal commonsense truth.

Attending the struggle to account for all complexities of a policy problem are not only pushback from powerful interests but also practical constraints. The policy sciences literature has acknowledged this challenge. McDougal et al. (1973) argued that policymakers and policy analysts need to negotiate a "barrage of sensory stimuli" (p. 369) at the individual cognitive and mechanical-analytical levels. This prescient statement anticipated the idea of socially constructed determinants of wicked problems, which were later theorized by critical policy scholarship and eventually in more mainstream scholarship, and fall both within and without the realm of measurability. For example, in applying Hofstede's (2001) four constructs of cultural values, Husted (2005) finds an association between capacity for sustainability and power distance, individualism versus collectivism, and masculinity versus femininity; these elements are not often present in econometric models but are instead explored in qualitative ways. At the same time, advancements in the capacity for measuring factors like cultural values, along with the development of analytical constructs to quantify and make policy-relevant meanings out of those elements, have brought softer contextual variables into mainstream econometric analysis. Lasswell saw this potential even before the technology revolution. In recognizing the potential of technology to improve the breadth and depth of policy analysis, Lasswell (1971a) argued that "the high speed computer has been ... a revolutionizing tool. In effect it allows a contextual, multi-valued ("philosophic") point of view to pass from fantasy and exhortation to reality" (p. 444). The same types of aspirational claims continue to be made for technological advancements like artificial intelligence (AI) and machine learning. The midcentury maturation of the policy sciences as a field saw a continued effort to understand reality in the holistic fashion advocated by Lasswell. For example, McDougal et al. maintained that interdependence as a characteristic of problems is often underappreciated. The crucial issue, then, is whether this lack of appreciation, to the extent that it still exists, compels policy analysts to double-down on technocratic modeling (in always assuming that Lasswell's "revolution" is imminent) or to expand the epistemological frame of inquiry in a way that acknowledges the categorical limitations of technology-based analytics overall.

Technology was expected by some to embed contextuality in policy analysis, but we argue that the embedding process has further tethered the policy sciences to a technocratic epistemic that views everything, even ambiguous context, as measurable, modellable, and ultimately predictable. Lasswell (1971a) cautioned against any narrow focus on problem causes (which we argue includes the narrowness of technocratic thinking), lest they lure analysts into "grandiose theories of unilinear evolution" (p. 443). The Janus-faced application of technology to complex problems is reflective at once of an ability to measure a wide range of variables and an interest in reinforcing the epistemics of quantifiability and instrumental rationalism. The ability to better quantify circumstantial factors appears to serve Lasswell's call for contextuality, but the tools of doing so (technology) are limited in their scope of vision while novel and advanced enough to be presented as suitably transformative. In this way, the tools falsely lure governments and publics into believing that public policy is rescued from its own narrow instrumentalist perspective and unilinear evolution by Lasswellian context finally done right. To escape the anachronism of contextual mismatch, public policy needs not to double-down on new technocratic capabilities but to liberate itself from them. The seeds of this epistemic transition lie (largely dormant) in the openness of Lasswell's vision for the intelligence function, hearkening to Deweyian pragmatism and countervailing instrumental rationalism's reductionist expropriation. The lingering question is whether this epistemic transition is able to withstand the epistemic chaos of the perfect storm and endure a soft or hard collapse. Lasswell's "open" intelligence function and its acknowledgment of diverse perspectives may provide the space for emergence, flexibility, evolution, and resilience in the face of unexpected contextual phenomena – but the same could have been said for the past century of policy practice, which has largely been epistemically rigid. The challenge, then, will be whether this openness continues to give effect to the loudest and most powerful ideas, which continue to reflect the legacy of instrumental rationalism.

While there may be an appetite among policy practitioners to develop a more holistic understanding about the determinants of wicked problems like climate change, including factors that test the limits of technocratic and rationalist perspectives, much academic thinking appears to remain mired in the theoretical and methodological territoriality that decades ago cleaved the study of public affairs into politics, policy, and administration (a path dependence begun, in the modern tradition, with the Weberian separation of politics and bureaucracy). Many academic efforts have targeted a reintegration of these intricately related subfields, beginning with Waldo (1952; see Svara [2008] for an overview) and well developed by post–New Public Management theories of administration such as New Public Administration (Frederickson, 1980) and New Public Service (Denhardt and Denhardt, 2000);

Howlett et al. (2017a) provide an overview and comparison of public administration paradigms and their relevance to comparative policy theory. The accordion effect of disciplinary disintegration and reintegration can be observed also in the organizational structure of the academic discipline itself. Farr et al. (2008) argue that discussions about policymaking are less frequent in political science and now gravitate "to schools of public policy mostly dominated by economists, where fundamental questions of power, politics, political institution-building, popular control, and practical leadership are neglected" (p. 29). The increasing presence of economic thinking in policy schools, the arguable consequence of a Trojan Horse effect in which policy studies looked to economics for more sophisticated quantitative methods but ended up embracing the field's broader epistemics, is a concern among those who argue that such thinking not only divorces the purity of theory from political realities but also dictates the terms of problem framing in areas beyond the scope of economic theory. According to Knott (2019), "while applied econometrics and political economy have come to play a prominent role in most schools of public policy and in the comprehensive policy schools, the field has become increasingly technocratic and difficult for practitioners to understand, let alone follow the scholarly books" (p. 89). Scholarly discussions about the influence of economic thinking in policy training date back at least to the 1970s, with a study by Ellwood (1981) that found an increasing presence of scholars with economics and business backgrounds in schools of policy and administration. The need to apply broader disciplinary and analytical frames to policy studies has not gone unnoticed, even by economics scholars themselves. In a survey of faculty at institutions affiliated with the Association for Public Policy Analysis and Management, Friedman (1991) found an interest among economists to apply course material more intensively to policy practice and to require noneconomics coursework (e.g., political science and sociology) in economics PhD curricula. In a more recent examination of trends in policy education, Anheier (2019a) argues that policy schools should "revisit the politics-analytics link by ... introducing political philosophy into core teaching to compensate for the normative vacuum and lack of vision in curricula dominated by political economy" (p. 75). Anheier further argues that the vision held by Lasswell of the "integrated school of policy" was never fully realized due to politicking and territoriality among university departments, a claim that may elicit little surprise from academics in most fields. A new Lasswell school focused on interdisciplinarity was proposed by Anheier (2019b) and may offer a vision for how the academy can prepare itself for a fundamental epistemic transition away from technocratic determinism and instrumental rationalism.

An additional element of the intelligence function is the provision and relevance of recommendations to policymakers by policy scientists. According to Lasswell (1951), "to some extent the quality of the intelligence function at any given time depends on the successful anticipation of policy needs before they have been generally recognized" (p. 5). Lasswell's conceptualization of this dimension of the intelligence function expressed the importance of foresight and prediction as characteristics of information gathering and analysis. Policy scientists who make recommendations based on foresight and prediction are not merely interpreters and conveyors of information but have power over the creation of knowledge and thus its content and meaning. Knowledge generated from the act of analyzing and prescribing policy – not only about a particular problem but about how to make policy itself – was envisioned as an input cycled back into the policymaking process. According to Dunn (2018a), "not only did [the policy sciences] mandate the creation of knowledge about the process of policymaking; they also required that the knowledge so created be used to improve that process." In this way, methods used to analyze a policy problem within a particular epistemic frame are designed and evaluated according to their own set of processes and criteria. Further, the feedback-based improvement process, genuine and empirically informed as it may seem in this case, is self-replicating. Epistemically bounded processes beget only a particular set of insights borne of the same mind-set and when fed back into the system reinforce the incumbent epistemic orientation in tautological fashion – a self-licking ice cream cone of epistemic navel-gazing. Marginal adjustments provide a case that improvement has been undertaken, convincing enough to forestall criticism of institutional stasis and epistemic sclerosis.

While technologically informed empiricism and increasingly sophisticated economic models seek to capture complexity in service to more contextualized and nuanced policy recommendations, many factors determining society's ability to address wicked problems are elusive of such tools; this caveat is strongly implied by the policy sciences through concepts like pragmatism and Lasswell's policy scientist of democracy. Efforts to understand how mainstream policy studies can embrace the more cautious and modest use of empiricist methods would benefit from rereading the foundational ideas of the policy sciences through the lens of contemporary policy problems and evolving scholarship about systemic complexity and social constructivism. However, the disruptiveness of post-empiricism – if a "new" epistemic[9] can be labeled at

---

[9] In referencing a new epistemic, we reject the idea that the old epistemic can be revived even in highly modified form. We embrace Lasswell's emphasis on context and his effort to reconcile facts and values but depart from those scholarly traditions that have used Lasswell's ideas to

all – outstrips the means of the staid analytical models to understand it, making epistemic change something that mainstream policy scholarship would struggle to meaningfully engage. Notably, this idea was implicitly foretold in early work by policy sciences scholars; Lasswell eschewed an overly technical approach to policymaking because, in the words of Dunn (2018b), "social processes define the context in which decision processes occur" (p. 115). According to this view, the recommendations of policy analysts serve as instruments for politically defined objectives such as sustainability and social equality, reflecting a decisional functionalism that gives policy its purpose. Even the seemingly objective work of policy analysts can be reinterpreted at any given stage of policymaking – a process as political at the agenda-setting stage as it is during implementation and evaluation. The tension between empirical analysis and political values is an evident characteristic of the intelligence function, particularly in the current era characterized by the convergence of two factors: (i) technocratic policy research that has high self-certitude and deep credibility among similarly minded policymakers, politicians, and agents of the power-knowledge nexus and (ii) populist political movements on both the political right (Edis, 2020) and left that challenge the credibility and legitimacy of a governance superstructure that appears monolithic and untouchably elite. For example, then-president of the United States Donald Trump both explicitly and subtly undermined the public credibility of health experts (including leading infectious disease expert Dr. Anthony Fauci) at the early stage of the COVID-19 outbreak in 2020, illustrating how tensions between science and politics can – when cynically exploited – compromise policy effectiveness.

3.3 Policy, Participation, and Power

Implicit in calls to develop more contextualized understandings about policy problems and solutions is the need to further democratize the policy process by accounting for a wider and more representative array of perspectives and inputs. A long-standing characteristic of the rationalist-technocratic policy project is its execution by a cadre of administrative, political, and scientific elites; in this way, the Frankfurt School argues that technocratic rationalism is fundamentally authoritarian. Even Lasswell's (1951) elaboration on the decision function articulates the importance of coordination and communication among researchers, advisors, and policymakers in generating "responsible interpretations . . . integrated with judgment" based on "authentic information"

---

establish a totalizing and synoptic (often but not exclusively technocratic) fundamentalism, even where participation and inclusivity are said to be guiding principles. The new epistemic warrants a novel way of thinking about how society understands problems but recognizes that some formative ideas in the policy sciences can be viewed as seeds for epistemic transformation.

(p. 5). Lasswell's later description of knowledge as "exercised by elites" (1971a; p. 446) recognizes that the privilege of naming and framing policy problems lies primarily among the politically powerful, many of whom received training in technocratic ways of thinking and governing from elite institutions. Such credentialing gives effect to the Bourdieuian *habitus* of technocratically professionalized policymakers and rank-and-file bureaucrats (Hartley and Ahmad, 2019). The implication that interpretations developed by knowledge elites is categorically "responsible" undermines Lasswell's emphasis on context, an understanding of which is possible only when moving beyond elite interpretations of policy problems. As such, we argue that the merits of Lasswell's work are to be appreciated individually, as they are not always mutually complementary; indeed, it is not necessary to wholly reject an intellectual tradition when identifying space for a new one, but to specify which existing ideas may fit with a new epistemology and which can be dismissed to the rubbish bin of failed ideas.

The putative hegemony of the technocratic elite is, from Lasswell's perspective, tempered by the policy scientist of democracy and implied by the stated preference of the policy sciences for interdisciplinarity over specialization (Farr et al., 2008). This preference hearkens back to Lasswell's complementary concept of the "cross-disciplinary manifold," which is said to have emerged during an era of rapid development in social sciences research in the early twentieth century (Dunn, 2019; Lasswell, 1971b). The call for interdisciplinarity is one reaction to what Lasswell described as fragmentation in constituent fields of the social sciences – a phenomenon extending from efforts to deepen disciplinary knowledge that (perhaps inadvertently) led to disengagement with broader practical context. An example is the field of economics and its segregation from political and policy contexts. At the same time, so-called knowledge creators – primarily in academic institutions – operate within the same type of fragmented and politicized environment as do many policy professionals; according to Lasswell (1971a), there is a "tendency to gang up against the innovator, especially the colleagues who utilize cross-field techniques or modes of thought" (p. 441). Such coercive pressure reflects a disciplinary elitism that goes beyond the lay-expert divide and undermines the ability of interdisciplinarity to exert its influence on policy practice. Further, the tempering effect implies a type of incrementalism that seeks to fold existing power structures into a new vision of participation and contextual sensitivity – a vision that is difficult to defend given the history of elite capture in both authoritarian and democratic settings. As such, the soft application of Lasswell's concept of the policy scientist of democracy again provides a satisfying enough counterbalance to forestall deeper criticism about elite influence while, conveniently enough for elites, changes little about underlying structures that perpetuate existing power imbalances. This we identify as one risk of retaining an intellectual legacy while searching for new epistemic pathways. The solution, then, is to be more critical and reflective about aspects of the policy sciences that appear to serve epistemic transition while perpetuating old ways of thinking; this involves an approach that is "radical" in the original sense of the word – revisiting unadulterated core ideas and re-routing their evolution toward a different epistemic vision. This epistemic transition is synonymous with what Berger and Esguerra (2017) describe as translation: "complex social and political processes in which new meanings are created and new relations forged, [involving] people and languages as much as material artefacts and . . . always fraught with relationships of power and domination" (p. 2).

From the applied perspective, the policy sciences see participatory mechanisms and their variants (e.g., co-production; Durose and Richardson, 2015) as necessary if not beneficial in the policymaking process. McDougal et al. (1973) argued that equal access to knowledge by "territorial and pluralistic groups" is essential for legitimizing the policymaking process and its outputs; without access to information, non-elites can be marginalized and their views "dismissed as the fruit of ignorance and bias" (p. 446). In this way, marginalization of the information, analytical capacity, and qualitative wisdom originating in non-elite sources politically sterilizes the practice of policymaking and forces the self-referential expert class to claim legitimacy based on in-group credentialing, coded communication and signaling, and power gestures. With a putative monopoly on capacities to generate data and monitor conditions about policy problems, this expert class engages in a performance of research that "may be carried on within an extremely rigorous normative framework" (McDougal et al., 1973; p. 368). Policy scientists, including McDougal and Lasswell, argued that this elite concentration of knowledge capacity and cursory solicitation or outright exclusion of input from external sources undermines the effectiveness of the intelligence function. It also compels elites to make increasingly contorted claims to legitimacy that focus on output legitimacy rather than process legitimacy (a characteristic common in authoritarian regimes and particularly in one-party or developmental states). We extend that argument to claim that elite concentration occurs even in ostensibly (but illusory) collaborative processes, such as co-production, in which persistent power imbalances are obscured by discourses about equity and equality in knowledge production. These structures ultimately serve an elite discourse on its own terms and offer a means for the power-knowledge nexus to deepen its hegemony by co-opting counter-hegemonic narratives (examples of which are the critically labeled processes of "greenwashing" (Delmas and Burbano, 2011; Laufer, 2003), "pinkwashing" (Lubitow and Davis, 2011), and "human rights washing" (Kuecker, 2014a).

Balancing elite and non-elite policymaking input in democratic systems during the current era of populism, climate skepticism, and general anti-technocracy implies a lingering tension that liberal models of governance struggle to resolve, particularly as the legitimation of democracy relies on the collective acceptance of what is true (for deeper discussions, see Porpora and Sekalala, 2019; Elkins and Norris, 2012; Estlund, 1993). Indeed, there exist technical dimensions of policymaking whose nuances are beyond the compre-hension of the untrained (e.g., fiscal, monetary, public health, climate, global trade, and other policy domains). While the duty of political communications is to distill such policy complexities into accessible language that helps citizens make informed voting decisions, scientific knowledge in both its original and lay-translated forms is an emergent battleground for political contestation and a convenient target for anti-elitism nested in narratives about freedom and individualism; an example is the "anti-mask" movement during the COVID-19 pandemic in the United States. McDougal et al. (1973) recognized this challenge in a prescient admonition relevant to debates about climate change and pandemic mitigation that emerged decades later: "in every society there are impatient or anti-intellectual elements who have no understanding of knowledge as a principal end ... it is no surprise that politicians in certain localities try to project a self-image of reassuring "folksiness" and to polemicize against the professional intellectual" (p. 412). Such a description invokes the long history of American anti-intellectualism (Hofstadter, 1963), as illustrated by an episode in which US Senator Jim Inhofe, a Republican Party member from Oklahoma, brought a snowball onto the floor of Congress in a widely ridiculed bid to prove that climate change was a hoax.[10]

The power-knowledge nexus faces an uncertain future in the populist post-truth era embodied by the Trump movement and other populist movements around the world and notably reflects declining interest in Enlightenment forms of truth (e.g., natural science) that typically legitimize policymaking. Categorical attacks on the credibility of science undermine the knowledge of experts, including technocrats, by destabilizing the epistemics of truth that produce and reproduce power. Examples of political threats to scientific narra-tives about policy problems are the perception of global climate policy as the project of a global "totalitarian" state or national climate policy as the project of anti-capitalist progressive elites; such claims are embraced as calls to action by skeptics, anti-globalists, economic protectionists, and anti-government

---

[10] https://edition.cnn.com/2015/02/26/politics/james-inhofe-snowball-climate-change/index.html

alarmists, among others. Efforts to understand climate skepticism and challenges to received narratives about policy problems cast the analytical gaze on
an ostensibly ill-informed and reactionary electorate, but such an analysis can
itself further entrench populist antipathy by reflecting an effort to measure and
manage resistance itself – potentially seen as both technocratic and politically
patronizing. McDougal et al. (1973) argued that "among the tribes or the castes
of many localities the inhabitants are well-aware of festering grievances that
may erupt in challenges to public order" (p. 377). The order in this case can be
manifest as an epistemic community (Dunlop, 2013; Haas, 1992) unaccount-
able to democratic systems but nevertheless bearing substantial influence on
policy while supporting its own credibility through claims to benevolence and
democratic openness.

Anti-technocratic sentiments, including those embodied by various forms of
populism left and right, have political implications for policies that address
wicked problems – including the post-2015 development agenda. If initiatives
to address global crises like climate change, macroeconomic instability, forced
migration, and pandemics represent at once liberal internationalism and technocratic policy, there is an inherent tension in the current geopolitical-economic
order that provides a clue for why policy has become dysfunctional in its
epistemic anachronism. The modern political zeitgeist in some countries
reflects a reactionary populist authoritarianism even while policy remains
wholly technocratic; as such, the fog of epistemic transition results from the
relative speed with which either populism or technocracy progresses (e.g.,
political preferences may shift more quickly than policy epistemics).
Regarding a third scenario, it is plausible that populism and technocracy
dovetail into an authoritarian techno-state in which the political narrative
embraces anti-elitism but policy decisions are still immune from political
influence in a way that serves powerful interests. The lingering influence of
technocracy amid an emerging epistemic liminality limits public policy's capacity to transition into a collapse and post-collapse era.

Understanding the lingering epistemic transition invites contemplation not
only of the tensions between technocracy and populism but also how reliance
on particular types of knowledge and information confounds efforts to define
and address policy problems. In examining the role of information in addressing wicked problems, it is necessary to consider the development, interpretation, and use of knowledge in the policymaking arena. Dunn and Holzner
(1988) argue that subjectivity, corrigibility, sociality, and complexity characterize how scientific and professional knowledge is applied to policy problems. The authors maintain that unresolved tensions exist within each factor
around contestability of framing, differing perspectives and goals, and

conflicting criteria (p. 3). The ability of political feedback systems to measure the proverbial "will of the people," the ability of policymakers to translate that will into policies, and the ability of bureaucrats to implement policies in service to desired outcomes are dependent in part on the structure of a sociopolitical ecology in which narratives advanced by elites become commonsense solutions in the fashion of Gramscian cultural hegemony; thus, these narratives elude popular assaults on their legitimacy (Caesar's wife is above suspicion) not through force but through a shared understanding that appears to originate with the victory of legitimate ideas. Dunn and Holzner's knowledge-society nexus is less a product of explicit manipulation by those in power (as we have suggested in the concept of the power-knowledge nexus) and more an expression of commonsense solutions to problems having characteristics plausible to lay audiences. An epistemic regime based on common sense, and one that is a product of forces endogenous to popular society, would appear more durable than one crafted and promoted only by the knowledge elite. A crucial question that may trouble policy elites, however, is whether scientifically calibrated and experimentally proven solutions developed in a sterile vacuum of rationalist empiricism are preferable to imperfect solutions having the popular credibility that accompanies democratic engagement (thus leading to the proverbial design-by-committee).

An additional question concerns not necessarily the element of elite preference but that of political acceptability; in the current era, it is plausible that popular input – or the impression thereof – is an indispensable ingredient for politically feasible policy. The efficacy of climate policy, for example, is contingent on reforms to the culture of consumption and the depths of hydrocarbons as the foundation of modern civilization. The culture of consumption defines society in the capitalist epoch and is so deeply engrained as common sense that meta-cognitive reflection beyond the poison arrows of bitter scholars is inconceivable, as is any revolutionary effort to crash the gates of the techno-rationalist epistemic fortress. Reminiscent of Foucault's governmentality, society disciplines its own actions by embracing a commonsense materialist narrative about how to measure personal happiness, quality of life, success, and human progress. The nexus of hydrocarbons and capitalism constitutes the essence of society, rendering efforts to decouple and deconstruct the two nearly impossible (Klein, 2015). The ultimate and persistently challenging task for technocratic and political elites has been to foster popular support for systems that economically benefit the few, including those that degrade the environment and exacerbate socioeconomic inequality. Policymakers, in their performance of Lasswell's intelligence function, have largely abetted this process knowingly or otherwise, but recent populist pushback is indication that this once roaringly successful scheme – for better and worse – faces an uncertain future.

Our discussion of foundational tenets in the policy sciences, including the intelligence function and its implications for the democratization of policy knowledge, illustrates that there persist anachronistic elements in how the field's theoretical legacies have been replicated and recast in service to particular arguments about technocracy, participatory governance, and others. It is not our intention to wholly and categorically ignore or dismiss the contributions of a century's worth of scholarship on the policy sciences and related topics. We seek instead to identify opportunities to freshen the policy sciences with a critical if optimistically anticipatory view on epistemic transition, recognizing from a practical perspective that new ideas must in some way meaningfully speak to the old – particularly in the highly networked and socialized sphere of academe. Further, we contend that the policy sciences are the most fruitful literature for such a discussion, as they have indeed sought and claimed to address (if imperfectly) manifold issues related to policymaking, from technocracy and knowledge creation to context and participation. In the coming era of epistemic instability, however, the policy sciences as a field either adapt and novelize or remain a safe harbor for legacy ideas and nostalgic thinkers. The future will move forward either way; we hope and anticipate that scholarship will follow suit. Relatedly, one element defining that future is the emergence in visibility and influence of so-called other knowledges, a matter to which this Element now turns.

3.4 De-Othering Other Knowledges

The technocratic view of policy problems implies a boundedness in the analytical unit, with context, uncertainties, and spillover effects confounding formal modeling efforts. This approach began to draw substantial criticism as it became evident that policy interventions were ineffective in the face of high complexity. Emerging from this critique were efforts to better capture the dimensions of wicked problems, with the aim either to rationalize and manage them or to acknowledge their intractability and "muddle through" (Lindblom, 1979). Wicked problems are said to elude full definition and have no clear solution. While the absence of a clear solution directs attention to the availability and effectiveness of analytical tools, the absence of a clear definition invites reflections about how problems are identified and defined. Variously conceptualized (e.g., as the intelligence function and agenda setting), problem definitions can be examined from two epistemic perspectives – rationalist and empiricist processes or contestable and interpretive processes. The former supports the self-certitude of de-politicized technocracy, while the latter implies constructed meanings developed through a negotiated and contested political process – as theorized by post-positivist scholarship and Marxian critiques of modernity, including Gramscian theories of hegemony, Foucault's notion of power and knowledge, the Frankfurt School's critical theory, and the diverse expanse of postcolonial theory. Our critique of public policy is informed by these theoretical approaches to power. While we could generate our line of inquiry using any of these as our focus, we find critical theory as developed by the Frankfurt School most pertinent because it illustrates best how the credibility accruing to rationalism marginalizes epistemics and knowledge systems that fall outside the scope of Enlightenment logic. We refer to these marginalized epistemics as "other knowledges."

Other knowledges are ways of thinking, doing, and being that take three central forms (see Kuecker, 2014b), each of which is mutually constituted by modernity – especially its rationalist epistemic. The first knowledge reflects the reality of being postcolonial. It is the knowledge created when the faltering promise of liberation leads to deepening understandings of power. The daily struggles of marginalized peoples are the source of the second form of other knowledge. According to Kuecker (2014b), "it is the knowledge about being human acquired from the internal conflicts and dilemmas of people in resistance" (p. 164). The third form of knowledge reflects the epistemologies and cosmologies of premodern societies that persist through modernity either in fragments or in their entirety. A significant portion of the global population may classify as having some form of other knowledge, as modernity's grasp has reached billions of people in diverse geographies and cultures over time. Those holding other knowledges include indigenous peoples, *mestiz@s*, and the descendants of enslaved peoples; a more expansive list might also include slum dwellers and migrants, and a still more expansive one might include all women.

Other knowledges imply an epistemic circumstantialism that is constituted by the Enlightenment's claims to universal knowledge or absolute truth, especially as that truth is articulated through public policy's dominant epistemic – instrumental rationalism – which perceives holders of other knowledge as social problem cases needing correction and modernization (Kuecker, 2017, 2014b). Application of the concept of the "other" suggests the colonial need to define and categorize something novel upon knowing it; accordingly, this process of constituting the other rests at the core of modern power, a point made by Said (1979) in *Orientalism* and pursued in the field of postcolonial studies. Public policy similarly problematizes other knowledges by constituting them as objects of corrective intervention. This process is embedded within a problem-framing exercise undertaken by many expressions of the intelligence function, casting other knowledge as a target for capacity building that results in the co-optation of other knowledges. The result is a "de-othering" of other knowledge.

The hegemony of instrumental rationalism, as the dominant epistemic foundation of policymaking revealing itself in how it treats society (including the other), operates through a coercion (Scott, 1998) that compels citizens to participate in activities that make them legible and measurable by the state. This data-substantiated normalization of behavior is an exercise in Foucauldian power and discipline, reducing qualitative differences to measurable dimensions visible only on technocratic terms (e.g., through demographic variables assigning ethnicity, religion, and gender). This coercive process is a soft marginalization of other knowledges, making unobserved differences invisible, epistemically erasing a vast store of social understanding and wisdom, and circumventing the very openness that participatory and democratic processes claim to support. According to McDougal et al. (1973), within the intelligence function "the criterion of openness is a commitment against monopoly and an endorsement of participation" (p. 376) – a view that underscores the role of diverse perspectives in policymaking. Nevertheless, efforts to de-other other knowledges (e.g., through narrative appropriation) may serve incumbent interests, as qualitative differences are reinterpreted in the language of prevailing epistemics and ultimately normalized, sanitized, or submerged.

Language used by early policy science scholars provides further insight into normative assumptions that may have led to othering in policy practice. Formative writings embraced the term "enlightenment" as a generic label for belief in rational and scientific epistemics having origins in the historical Enlightenment. In applying this label, scholars were able to add both cultural and geographical properties to comparisons of policy practice; concepts like "development" and "modernization" have been similarly applied to dualistic analytical sorting of countries and societies. According to McDougal et al. (1973), "the global stock of enlightenment is not equally dispersed ... large sections of the world must still be characterized as an enlightenment wilderness almost wholly out of touch with contemporary science" (p. 411). The tone of such pronouncements can be seen as constitutive of Enlightenment-based policy practice while exclusionary of other knowledges, a form of intellectual neocolonialism seeking to modernize the other as a mandate of "development." In a call to universalize enlightenment or Enlightenment ideals, which policy scientists saw as a crucial step in liberating hinterland societies from what they perceived to be the regressive illogics of traditionalism, McDougal et al. later maintained that "there must be a strong demand for the sharing of enlightenment, and skill and power must not be used to restrict this diffusion" (p. 443). Rather than viewing the coercive dissemination of rationalist epistemics as a gesture of enlightenment power, the prevailing perspective in the policy sciences appeared to implicate some other power as the proverbial Horatius at the bridge preventing dissemination of science, common sense, and enlightenment thinking. This view seems to contradict the policy sciences' promotion of inclusion and its distaste for hegemony.

Given the recently increasing global interconnectedness of policy dialogues and understandings, in particular through epistemic communities and issue-specific networks concerning development and sustainability, "enlightenment transfer" is now less a geographic phenomenon than a networked one. Such as there is a global enlightenment movement or cohesive development community, it stands as an institutionalized phenomenon advanced by multilateral agencies, NGOs, international financial institutions, consultancies serving these previously mentioned entities, and scholarly networks emerging from the internationalization of higher education and research. This mix of actors constitutes a diverse, influential, and well-resourced epistemic community shaping enlightenment proselytization that pushes best practices in political, economic, and social reform and now increasingly in sustainability and smartness. Notably, McDougal et al. (1973) advocated for "checks on information monopolies . . . by the establishment of world networks of scientific laboratories and universities controlled by international organizations" (p. 443). However, those putative checks on monopoly have themselves congealed into a monopoly, as the global governance landscape of McDougal's early 1970s bears scant resemblance to that of the 2020s in context and problem framing.

The argument that global networks of knowledge creators and policy thought leaders could impede rather than perpetuate elite capture and exclusionary practices must have seemed novel and even plausible in prior epochs. In the current era, however, the argument invites critical reflection. So thoroughly has rationalism embedded its epistemic in ways of thinking, being, and researching shared by global institutions – founded and funded largely by wealthy Western countries – that the concept of a fluid global network receptive to other knowledges belies observable reality. The received wisdom about development and sustainability is supported by an information monopoly within structures and institutions that were designed at the height of mid-century rationalist-solutionism. This wisdom was reshaped to accommodate ideological transition away from government intervention (e.g., Keynesianism) and toward neoliberal reform ideas and has ultimately settled into a stable state in which instrumental rationalism is mainstream common sense. Efforts by global organizations to signal a democratization of knowledge gathering and sharing, particularly through participatory feedback processes and crowdsourcing of information, aim to localize and politically legitimize a centralized policy effort. As illustrated through Arnstein's (1969) ladder of engagement, such efforts can be categorized more as passive informing and coercion than as meaningful participation or co-production. Relatedly, McDougal et al. (1973) argued that in the feedback process, some participants with potentially useful knowledge may not be forthcoming or assertive because they do not view themselves as "equal participants in the community process or are ... ambivalent in regard to all authority" (p. 377). Given the recent rise of right-wing populist-majoritarian skepticism and distrust of government authority in many countries, it may be expected that historically marginalized other knowledges would self-censor within the intelligence function. This intentional auto-marginalization could be seen as a form of survival – an effort to avoid submitting to processes that make the other legible and thereby vulnerable to the forces actively or subliminally protecting enlightenment hegemony. Taken a step further, this could be considered a form of epistemic resistance by dissociation or withdrawal. It can also be considered a proactive assertion of autonomy, reflecting a desire to claim the right to decide based on other knowledge and not the knowledge held by the World Bank or other policy agents.

Facing the power of public policy and its institutional structures, marginalized groups holding other knowledges must strategize how to respond. We can observe a continuum of responses ranging from reactive to proactive and mirroring social behavior from restorationist to revolutionary. The Zapatista indigenous rebellion in Chiapas, Mexico, provides an example of a proactive and revolutionary strategy that rejects the neocolonial power of public policy as articulated in state development assistance and similar projects originating with nongovernment organizations. This rejection is based on the Zapatistas' intentional autonomy, which aims to transform modern constructs of power by siting the "right to decide" within indigenous communities (Kuecker, 2017, 2014b). Their efforts reflect a strategy to operate outside the box of public policy's power to constitute the other. On the opposite end of the spectrum, we observe those whose resistance strategy leads to work inside the box, perhaps with the goal of using the proverbial master's tools to disassemble the master's house. Slum Dwellers International (SDI) is an example, as illustrated in Satterthwaite's (2001) discussion of the organization's interactions with the nexus of international development community actors. SDI works directly with the nexus in an attempt to leverage public policy's co-production outreach to the other. In this way, SDI becomes de-othered, part of the development community nexus as manifest by its co-opted presence at the neocolonial exhibit halls of UN Habitat's World Urban Forum. SDI is successful in elevating its voice within the global public policy community, but this is done on the latter's conditions and terms; indeed, program funding is contingent often on conforming to the development narrative, especially through the demonstration of tangible best practices that fit the inset boxes of annual reports. The Zapatistas, by contrast, refuse to participate in such events, preferring to create their own gatherings at their own venues on their own terms. Zapatista attempts to subvert technocratic rationalism constituted a threat to the nexus of development power and its effort to de-other the other, provoking an extended counterinsurgency offensive that deployed paramilitary violence; this is evident in the escalating frequency of attacks on Zapatista communities throughout 2020.

We close Section 3 by briefly considering the role of technology in elevating or squelching knowledge in its many forms. Lasswell (1971a) argued that technology enables "all participants in the social process to engage in a continuing intelligence and appraisal activity designed to re-define policy objectives and strategies" (p. 445). Decades later and in the midst of a raging digital transformation, it is clear how this idea could have originated from quixotic expectations about socio-technical systems – but it is also clear that in practice Lasswell's idea as he originally envisioned it has not met these high expectations. The hope that technology would facilitate the democratization of information has materialized in episodic cases; for example, e-governance systems have brought some policy functions closer to citizens and have improved the efficiency, effectiveness, and transparency of public services in particular ways (Dawes, 2008). At the same time, it is appropriate to contemplate the use of technology as a form of Arnstein's (1969) tokenism: the capacity to solicit input from citizens about policy initiatives, as a democratic box to check, has been simplified and superficially legitimized through technology. It is not apparent, however, that this capacity has loosened the narrative grip of the power-knowledge nexus. Gaps in access to technology, particularly across generational, socioeconomic, and geographic dimensions, prevent it from realizing Lasswell's vision of engaging "all participants in the social process." Additionally, while technology has made information more widely and quickly available, vulnerabilities to content quality and legitimacy undermine the construction of truth (e.g., the phenomenon of and rhetoric around "fake news"; Hartley and Vu, 2020; Lazer et al., 2018). The Internet can be seen as a public square, commons, free market of ideas, or republic of ideas – and thereby as a construct of communicative action in the Habermasian mold (Geiger, 2009; Heng and De Moor, 2003). As such, it facilitates the democratization and circulation of ideas while undermining the dominance of prevailing narratives. This comes at a cost to sociopolitical stability, as technologies are agnostic to human values: for example, American white nationalism and aggrieved ethnic majoritarianism have as much access to the virtual commons as do the movements of marginalized communities or the pronouncements of the scientific community. As availability is no indicator of validity, the responsibility for interpretation falls to the consumer of information. Accordingly, the deinstitutionalization of information access is a profoundly disruptive moment for the business of claiming truth. As such, technology can be seen as a facilitator of the power-knowledge nexus and a threat to its hegemony, both in the context of political pushback and in the context of resistance by holders of other knowledges; indeed, it reflects another way in which the basis of knowledge is becoming fragmented in a process that has the potential to enlarge political space for marginalized understandings and alternative epistemics.

4 Epistemic Liminality

In Section 2, we established the proposition that society is experiencing a soft collapse, and in Section 3, we revisited Lasswell's pragmatism to contemplate public policy's moment of reckoning amid systemic disruption and contextual instability. In Section 4, we examine systemic transition and its implications for how public policy is understood and practiced. We use this line of inquiry to propose a research agenda that recognizes the contextual and epistemic instability that will likely characterize the twenty-first century. The argument proposes that public policy's dominant epistemic, instrumental rationalism, becomes increasingly anachronistic during the epistemic transition while also retaining a firm grasp on public policy's intelligence function. The implication is that a transition from one system or way of thinking to another includes a liminal state between the two. The nature and duration of this liminal state are determined in part by the scale of the system; micro systems experience fast-paced, short transitions where a definitive tipping point brings an abrupt change to the new system, while macro systems like the construct of modernity have slow-burning, lengthy transitions that may be less perceptible except during moments of crisis that signal deeper flaws and processes of change. We argue that modernity is in the throes of a decades-long collapse-driven transition that will define the twenty-first century. Throughout this extended period of liminality and accompanying epistemic instability, old ways of thinking will persist despite their evident anachronisms while new forms of thinking will be slow to materialize and will meet immense pushback. The dominance and collectively agreed common sense of the old epistemic will obscure and discredit the new epistemic even as it emerges from the convergence of undeniable realities; this process is responsible for public policy's mismatch with the contemporary context of systemic transition. Macro transitions tend toward instability as a system oscillates between reproduction and collapse amid liminality, punctuated by crisis events such as the 2020 pandemic that confound existing thinking and legacy constructs of public policy.

In advancing a research agenda, Section 4 first outlines three epistemic modes of thinking present in the liminal state and how they address wicked problems; it then applies these modes to three theories of policy change. The epistemic modes examined are technocratic thinking (an instrumental-rationalist perspective supported and deepened by advanced technical capabilities), Frankfurt thinking (a theoretical perspective concerning narrative hegemony and marginalization), and predicament thinking (a practical or pragmatic perspective rooted in the policy sciences); the three frames of policy change are multiple streams, advocacy coalition, and punctuated equilibrium. Our goal is to invite scholarly contemplation about novel policy epistemics that may emerge from the liminal state. While not explicitly predictive, our discussion aims to encourage research about the degree to which society is capable of transcending public policy's anachronistic epistemic with the goal of identifying theoretical space for an emerging epistemic that is currently unknowable. This process of epistemic transition and transcendence can be seen as a form of translation (Berger and Esguerra, 2017); specifically, it raises questions about how policy translates from a self-assured anachronism to a more epistemically humble unknowable. This introductory section establishes a basis for our overlay of modes of thinking onto theories of policy change by discussing the dynamics of public policy and wicked problems in the liminal state.

Wicked problems tax the solution-focused policy epistemic. An illustration is offered by the Indian Institute for Human Settlements in a summary of the IPCC Special Report (Bazaz et al. 2018): "exceeding the 1.5°C global warming limit, even if only temporarily, will lead us into a highly uncertain world. Such an overshoot will push a number of natural and human systems beyond their limits of adaptation and into possible futures about which we have limited scientific knowledge and no institutional or governance experience" (p. 11). Scholarship across multiple disciplines provides a variety of conceptual and theoretical frames for understanding how such uncertainty destabilizes established ways of thinking, including Rittel and Webber's (1973) wicked problems, Peters's (2018, 2017, 2005) complex problems (as opposed to merely "complicated" problems), and Bennett and Lemoine's (2014) VUCA (volatility, uncertainty, complexity, and ambiguity, as conceptualized within a business management frame).

Due to the elusive nature of wicked problems as an object of analysis, academic scholarship has failed to arrive at a consensus understanding about the implications of wicked problems amid epistemic contestation and instability. Even those studies focusing specifically on climate change and related policy adaptation suffer from what Dupuis and Biesbroek (2013) call the "dependent variable problem" (definitional ambiguity in the outcome), suggesting an epistemic crisis deepening as wicked problems converge to push society beyond a critical threshold and into a soft collapse. As the old epistemic seeks to fortify its credibility amid cascading policy failures, a new epistemic has yet to emerge to replace it. This period of liminality is characterized by an epistemic fog that destabilizes not only the self-evident truths of Enlightenment thinking but also the power structures in which epistemic conservatives rhetorically manipulate these truths to claim governing legitimacy amid the rise of other knowledges.

The salience of wicked problems is a matter well familiar to environmental studies, particularly in literature addressing the climate predicament (Hopson and Cram 2018; Defries and Nagendra 2017; Pryshlakivsky and Searcy 2013; Murphy 2012). This literature suggests that applying rationalist policy solutions to wicked problems is a challenge reminiscent of the proverbial Gordian knot, as wicked problems in their interconnectedness and wide-ranging set of determinants defy reductionist social science focused on discrete definitions and solutions. Given that policy in its normative capacity is focused on problem resolution, the uncertain futures implied by wicked problems and liminality more generally require open-ended approaches to conceptualizing policy solutions. Relatedly, Ackoff (2010) provides a taxonomy for understanding approaches to policy problems: *absolution* (denial of responsibility), *resolution* (relying on familiar and path-dependent interventions), *solution* (proactive consideration for how to address a problem), and *dissolution* (reshaping or recontextualizing the problem until it disappears). The implication for policy targeting wicked problems, which Ackoff argues are best addressed through dissolution, is that the solution – such as one exists in a complete sense – is both unknowable until it has been applied and contingent on related policies. In an epistemic sense, this argument (productively) undermines public policy's methodological focus on conclusive foresight and deterministic planning. As wicked problems converge into systemic crises in the twenty-first century and constitute the liminal state of transition, the instrumental-rationalist model of policy intervention is increasingly outmatched, without any clear substitute. We turn now to three modes of thinking about policy problems, to illuminate finer points across the universe of epistemic approaches.

4.1 Technocratic Thinking

In discussing technocratic thinking, we begin with a semantic distinction between the concept and "technology" thinking. Technocratic thinking is a methodological ideology articulated through the rationalist-instrumentalist mind-set (technology-based or otherwise) and is frequently embraced and shaped by experts and policymakers. Technology thinking is an interpretive orientation concerning the effects of technology on society, often as a matter of policy interest. Both are linked, with the emergence of increasingly sophisticated technologies giving deeper effect to technocratic thinking by providing capacities to measure, monitor, and analyze a wider array of human experiences and natural phenomena. We proceed with the term "technocratic thinking" as it relates more closely to our argument about epistemic liminality and transition. The literature on technocracy is well developed and requires no elaboration here; for overviews and critiques, see Friedman (2019) and Burris (1993). Accordingly, this Element's preceding discussion of instrumental rationalism indicts technocratic thinking as an epistemic that has dominated more than a century of policymaking and continues to shape narratives about wicked problems. As such, this subsection focuses not on relitigating the perils of technocratic thinking per se but on pondering the implications of new generations of technological change for the persistence of technocratic thinking as a mode of policy framing in the liminal state and whether it can influence an emergent epistemic. Further, we maintain that two major disruptive technologies – AI and bioengineering – accompany a soft collapse that will likely bear the emergent properties characterizing states of liminality. In this section, we focus on AI while calling for additional research about the role of bioengineering in the emergence of a new epistemic.

There is high disruptive potential borne by the information technology revolution, embodied in advancements in not only AI but also big data, algorithms, machine learning, and others. The information technology revolution is precipitating deep changes within the substructures and superstructures of society – from personal interactions to global structural dynamics in employment – and policy is an integral factor in these forces. It is therefore incumbent on future-ready policymaking to negotiate the unpredictable societal impacts of the technology revolution and to rethink a governing environment in which data and analytics are substantiating and perpetuating instrumental rationalism. For example, AI's influence on environmental policy is increasingly consequential (see Ye et al. [2020] for a review concerning pollution controls); an example is the use of big data and ecosystem monitoring in "Environmental Decision Support Systems" (Cortés et al., 2000) and the increasing popularity of "smart water management" (Hartley and Kuecker, 2020). A lingering question is whether and when AI will evolve to the degree that machines eclipse humans in the ability to conduct deep analysis related to environmental policy, and whether this evolution will usher instrumental rationalism into a new era of epistemic dominance and self-certitude or render it humanly incomprehensible and thus dismissed to the realm of technological esoterica and science fiction.

In work that supports this argument about epistemic and systemic transition, Du Sautoy (2019) postulates that machines will dramatically transition from learning to innovation, a development that may take some policymaking tasks out of the hands of human experts; this once seemingly absurd notion is now an increasingly plausible extension of rationalism to its furthest reaches. A principal advantage of AI is that it can execute work without vulnerabilities such as human error, bias, or corruption. Nevertheless, concerns persist that inequities and inequalities are embedded in humanly designed algorithms (Christian, 2020; Benjamin, 2019; Zuboff, 2019; Eubanks, 2018; Noble, 2018; O'Neil, 2016); Barth and Arnold (1999), in research published relatively early in the AI era, provide an overview of this debate that remains relevant. The implications of AI for policy practice are unpredictable but could include a doubling-down on technocratic thinking and a Luddite populist pushback against not only the tools of instrumental rationalism but also its conceptual basis and exclusionary form of expertise. The transition, in whatever way it manifests itself, may likewise lead to a fundamental reworking of the Enlightenment notion of human agency (Harari, 2018), especially the claim long embraced by classical economists and some policy scholars that individual rationalism bound by effective institutions leads to collectively optimal outcomes. Technology-driven disruption, in its manifold forms, is likely to be a major driver of twenty-first-century epistemic instability and may further call into question the premises of modernity's truth claims as the basis of policy expertise and authority.

The impact of AI presents substantial challenges to the viability of outputs from legacy models used by the mainstream policy intelligence function. The concept of "intelligence," as long operationalized in the policy sciences, is one in which humans are the agents – an idea reflective of Enlightenment modernism and its humanist tradition. By contrast, AI introduces the concept of "machines as agents," thereby altering received understandings about human agency. Curiously, AI can be considered a purer embodiment of instrumental rationalism in its putative immunity from human bias (to the degree that such bias is not engineered into AI itself), and it is possible to envision a future in which AI is capable of doing all five "intelligence tasks" outlined by McDougal et al. (1972). As an alternative form of agency and intelligence, AI has multiple plausible development trajectories from solutionism to wholesale ontological disruption; in the current liminal state, the emergence and influence of AI are ongoing and difficult to foresee. Two such trajectories appear paramount: to be a cause of or solution to global crises and to be a fundamental disruption to the ontology of what it means to be human. In the latter, the Enlightenment notion of the human as the world's apex agent cedes to a new epoch where humanity struggles to adapt to shifting existential contexts. That AI will serve as a partner complementing rather than replacing human agency is an optimistic projection; stress, uncertainty, and dislocation in the transformation of what it means to be human appear at least as likely. As instrumental rationalism predisposes society to see technology as a tool for human purposes, AI marches forward amid a potentially tragic underestimation of what happens when humans are no longer the only agents. Understanding how truth, intelligence, human agency, and political legitimacy converge in such emerging contexts can help structure discussions about epistemic liminality, including those induced by change in technology and natural systems. Policymaking under a scenario in which machines are members of the public, constructors of their own intelligence, and agents of the ultimate "other knowledge" is not a laughable fantasy but a possibility that invites serious scholarly inquiry and illuminates frontiers for reviving and refashioning the policy sciences and policymaking itself. As the "after-modern" policy epistemic will be constituted essentially by the human-machine relationship, policy practitioners should prepare for the imminence of post-human policy while policy scholars should research and debate how the post-human society might look.

4.2 Frankfurt Thinking

While AI pathways invite deeper scholarly contemplation about post-human public policy as an emergent epistemic in the liminal state, this section invites contemplation about the persistent dominance of instrumental rationalism in the liminal state and its potential to shape an emerging epistemic that reproduces the current tensions between mainstream public policy and other knowledges as previously discussed. Adorno and Horkheimer's (2002 [1945]) *Dialectic of Enlightenment* describes Enlightenment rationalism as an effort to liberate knowledge from the clutches of myth, fantasy, and tradition – which the authors frame in more poetic terms as a modernist disenchantment with the enchanted world (ideas that had been used previously by Weber (1978 [1921]); further discussion in Alexander, 2013). To overcome the alienation of disenchantment and modernity's "dark side," the Frankfurt School proposed critical theory as the path toward a re-enchanting liberation. The persistence of technocratic rationalism in the liminal state, according to this view, would facilitate the continued marginalization, co-optation, and erasure of other knowledges that constitute the array of emergent epistemics. Frankfurt thinking invites scholars to continue deploying the multiple currents of critical theory in centering and

visibilizing other knowledges and in creating space for the autonomous liberation of epistemic emergence that eschews the AI path of post-humanism in
favor of a fresh form of self-deterministic humanism. By enhancing its understanding of other knowledges (Barth, 1995), a new policy epistemic would
recognize ways of being, seeing, thinking, and acting that exist autonomously
from the modern rationalist epistemic. These ways, for example, are those of
peoples and societies (e.g., Indigenous, migrants, peasants, the geographically
isolated, and people of color) who have been marginalized if not erased by
modernity. The other knowledges of the enchanted world, as explored by
postcolonial literature on cultural discourses and semiotics (Mignolo, 2000),
include neglected practices and conceptualizations of being that have evolved
over long arcs of time and in accordance with shifting ecosystems.

Our first example of other knowledges serving as a potential emergent
epistemic comes from Hershock's (2006) reading of policy issues through the
lens of Buddhism, in particular the concept of public goods and their manifestation in local and global settings with high interdependence. Hershock shows
how Buddhist notions of interdependence can lead to heightened equality and
equity in policy areas like health, education, and development. With 2,500 years
of thought history, Buddhism's way of seeing is, according to Hershock, well
suited for twenty-first century challenges.

Positioning away from Western scholars advocating for non-Western epistemics, we turn to Smith's (2012) *Decolonizing Methodologies* as a second
example. Smith argues for a radical break from the dominance and power of
Western perspectives by abolishing their compromised research methods in
favor of other knowledge driven by organic and autonomous methods.
Importantly, Smith's perspective as a Maori women recognizes how modernity
constitutes her knowledge as the "other" while exemplifying cultural recovery,
reassertion, persistence, and resistance. Smith's work builds on a long tradition
of postcolonial studies, in which thinkers including Said, Fanon, and Ngugi Wa
Thiong seek to liberate epistemic thought from the colonialist fate of being
viewed as the "other."

A third example comes from South Asian perspectives in subaltern studies,
which build on Gramsci's conceptualization of subaltern groups to escape the
construct of the other and reclaim the history of subordinate groups. Led by
Indian scholars Guha and Spivak, subaltern studies had a profound impact in
pushing postcolonial studies toward a radical critique of the modern epistemic.
In Latin American studies, for example, historians battled over a perceived
usurpation of subaltern studies by Anglo scholars from the United States (see
responses to Mallon, 1994), while a group of scholars from Latin America led
by Dussel and including Escobar (2011), Grosfoguel, Mignolo, and Quijano

proposed "transmodernity" as a way to escape the coloniality of power. Finally, we offer the example of a self-described de-professionalized academic, Esteva, who joins the postcolonial embrace of post-development critiques of instrumental rationalism. Esteva's research advocates for sociocultural autonomy through the retention of Indigenous cosmologies in what he and Prakash (1998) label "grassroots postmodernism."

This small sampling of postcolonial scholarship represents a range of other knowledges that are epistemically seen by Frankfurt thinking, potentially active within the liminal state, and have potential to constitute an emergent epistemic that contests or coexists with modernity's instrumental rationalism. Further research is needed to vet these epistemic pathways and possibilities, particularly regarding the willingness and ability of public policy to yield the dominance of instrumental rationalism to historically superordinate other knowledges through a paradigm-shifting re-enchantment. The empiricism of Enlightenment rationalism, however, is so deeply allied with modern policy logic that any such re-enchantment – from collaborative and accommodative to wholly iconoclastic – would likely struggle against pearl-clutching accusations of de-empiricization. Further, there is no clear path to re-enchantment as verbalized by the epistemics of rationalist policy – indeed, one of its self-preserving properties. Notions of co-production and participation offer a conveniently superficial image of policymaking liberalization without the need to abandon underlying epistemics. Thus, the concept of a re-enchanted approach to policy presents an unresolvable paradox because it would transcend and confound ossified epistemic boundaries; the result of re-enchantment may indeed not be public policy as it is currently understood. A wholly revolutionary epistemic would likely produce outcomes that elude rationalist measurement and understandings, a phenomenon itself embodying the very term "enchantment" in its departure from de-enchanted enlightenment. Premodern or a-modern ways of thinking, being, and doing had survived for millennia or longer before being reshaped, reconstituted, and reinterpreted by rationalist-empiricist language and narratives that valorize Enlightenment modernity as a commonsense construct. At a practical operational level, progress towards transformation on this scale would require the promotion of subaltern forms of what non-subaltern modernism understands to be policymaking – for example, through autonomous approaches to knowledge production advocated by Smith, Esteva and Prakash, and others as previously mentioned.

The store of other knowledges is vast and offers insights of incalculable value. It is forged through a long temporal horizon of what rationalism would label adaptation, evolution, and natural experimentation. However, there is a trap at the intersection of the modern epistemic and the multitude of other knowledges: even a seemingly inclusive public policy approach seeks to instrumentalize and leverage other knowledge. This approach risks reproducing neocolonial power inequities that institutionalize subaltern groups while claiming to serve them. A research agenda driven by a true "epistemology of questioning" (Homer-Dixon, 2006) would need to deconstruct and purge meta-narratives and normative concepts laden with power imbalances (e.g., development and sustainable development) and engage in a hard reckoning about the neoliberalization of participatory politics and the inability of "progressive" concepts like inclusiveness, collaboration, and variants (e.g., co-production; Cooke, 2001) to unseat the dominant epistemic. While analytical neutrality would avoid romanticizing a supposed "languid placidity" of other knowledges, it is imperative to acknowledge the appropriative risks of neoliberal multiculturalism and their embodiment in concepts like *Indio permitido* – the "acceptable/permitted Indian" (Hale, 2004). Participatory approaches to development often harbor an illusion of participation that obscures the perpetuation of neocolonial power and knowledge structures (Li, 2007; Ferguson, 1994). The operational understanding of inclusion appears to assume that Enlightenment rationalism is the default norm by which other knowledges are selectively mined for insight and against which their value is judged. Until public policy redresses these sins of commission by critically interrogating the power-knowledge nexus, the inclusion of-other knowledges in policy processes will be fraught, paradoxically, with the risk of continued marginalization under any epistemic eventuality following the liminal state.

While constitutive of the rationalist power-knowledge nexus that legitimizes public policy and facilitates the marginalization of other knowledges, appeals to common sense as a normalizing force are deeply embedded within policy's claims and methods. The narrative of rationalism shapes norms and in the process privileges certain thought systems without needing to appear defensive or protectionist in marginalizing alternative thought systems. The resulting invisibility explains the discursive silences of commonsense policy language, especially the way policy indulgently assumes the objectivity of its subjective and value-laden propositions (e.g., in the promotion of neoliberal and market-based governance models). The subtle power of commonsense policy narratives is that they need no top-down effort to build socially and culturally constructed (or endogenous) understandings of reality; they materialize and endure with little more than passive influence, once the terms of the discourse are decided. The appeal of rationalism is endemic not only at policy and societal levels but also in how Enlightenment thinking shapes individual beliefs and behavior. To paraphrase the Chinese philosopher Lao Tzu, a commonsense policy best serves its purpose when people barely know that it exists, and when its outcomes are met the people say they did it themselves. This idea is at the heart of Foucault's (2007 [1977–1978]) concept of "governmentality," the subtle and passive control of human behavior needing no formal force and expressing itself through diffuse models such as self-government – a phenomenon having invited decades of scholarship about the ubiquitous influence of neoliberalism. As an illustration, we consider Agrawal and Bauer's (2005) application of Foucault's governmentality to environmental policy in India, which shows how "environmentality" converges knowledge and governance to constitute environmental subjects. A more recent example comes from a study of global crises, in which De Roeck (2019) applies governmentality to a study of power relations within the European Union's climate change adaptation efforts, which "promote the production of quantified and depoliticized knowledge" (p. 160). We take the term "depoliticized" to mean a process in which participation is absent, and together with "quantified" to imply the preeminence of elite narratives in shaping public policy.

Among the most successful commonsense policy narratives, and one directly related to the sustainability challenge, is capitalism. Within public policy, capitalism's underlying assumptions are rarely interrogated beyond what flavor of capital the public deserves – statist or neoliberal. Nevertheless, there are notable critics, even anti-capitalists, who rebelled against the dominance of instrumental rationalism's intimate embrace of capitalism. David Korten, for example, earned a PhD in economics from Stanford, taught at Harvard Business School, and served for fifteen years as a top development officer for the United States Agency for International Development and for the Ford Foundation in Indonesia. He came to realize that he was killing cultures and left the world of policy to expose the system. In *When Corporations Rule the World* (1998), he identifies neoliberal globalization and corporate power as the culprit, while in the sequel, *The Post Corporate World* (1999), he identifies capitalism as the "cancer" killing society and the ecosystem. Preceding Korten was Herman Daly, who served as senior economist at the World Bank and later advanced a radical vision for steady-state economics that countered capitalism's unstainable need for perpetual growth (Daly, 1991). Similarly, non-Western thinkers like Walden Bello operated on the mainstream path before turning critical. Bello, a PhD in sociology from Princeton University, was "radicalized" through his field research in Chile during President Salvador Allende's short-lived movement toward socialism. Bello returned to the Philippines to fight against the profoundly corrupt and destructive dictatorship of Ferdinand Marcos, which led him to expose the role of International Monetary Fund and World Bank policies in supporting the regime. Bello co-founded a research institute in Bangkok, named Focus on the Global South, that further exposed the ills and follies of development policy. The sociopolitical context that supports capitalist manifestations of the power-knowledge nexus may now be giving way to a turbulent new era of contestation, exposure, debate, and plausible alternatives. Policy scholars should engage this debate, especially as the prospects of climate change and systemic collapse, in addition to growing economic inequality and social injustice, generate popular concern in societies where dissent is tolerated. The "problem of capital" will arguably define the future of environmental policy and that of society more broadly, with destabilizing effects on the hegemony of legacy policy epistemics and commonsense modes of thinking.

In closing this section, we propose that Frankfurt thinking's research agenda focus on three lines of inquiry. First, it should deploy critical theory in exploration of the ways technocratic rationalism might retain its dominance in public policy and endure the transition from liminality to what comes thereafter. Second, it should consider the implications for public policy if other knowledges survive the perfect storm of a soft collapse and emerge as a rival or dominant epistemic. Third, Frankfurt thinking invites the policy field to shift its research frameworks away from modernity's dualities between technocratic rationalism and other knowledges and toward identifying new systems of thought emerging from the liminal state. In this section, we have not explicitly advocated for other knowledges but, as a call to the academy, have encouraged a broader orientation to enable the field's recognition of rival epistemics – as they might emerge. We argue that systemic instability and liminality, as equalizers of epistemic validity, mandate such an orientation.

4.3 Predicament Thinking

In a soft collapse–driven liminal state, humanity faces multiple predicaments but the dominance of technocratic rationalism within the public policy epistemic leads most predicaments to be either overseen or dismissed as manageable. We understand predicaments to be situations that have no clear path for optimal resolution, forcing policymakers to select suboptimal paths with costly trade-offs. As such, predicament thinking can be seen as the epistemic of tough choices. It is a perspective that acknowledges unresolved problems that are potentially permanent, exist within contexts that will experience long-term disruption (e.g., those resulting from a changing ecosystem or climate), and require paradigm shifts in policy epistemics that may be unlikely or infeasible. One example of an attempted paradigm shift in a predicament-based situation was Ecuador's effort to reduce carbon emissions, a policy in which the government redefined the economic potential of its oil reserves by promising to not extract the oil in exchange for a sovereign wealth fund paid for by the global community (the "oil in the soil" program and associated paradigm shift faltered, however, due to an operational dispute over control of the fund; Martin, 2011). In this case, Ecuador faced a choice between the destructive path of resource extraction and the neocolonial terms of a sovereign wealth fund that undermined the country's sovereignty. Predicament thinking informs the type of policy that prepares for or lessens the severity of crises, with policymakers developing and choosing from a set of unattractive options. This approach represents an epistemic shift away from the instrumental-rationalist belief in the efficacy of perfectly designed or calibrated policy tools for solving problems. Rather than solving the problem, predicament thinking manages it.

Characterizing the context of policy predicaments is an interconnectedness that frustrates rationalist logics that reduce complexity to discrete, measurable, linear, and solvable problem constructs. Hershock's (2006) call for deploying Buddhist epistemics in policy framing is derived largely from a focus on interconnectedness that would drive policy toward mitigation over solutionism. In a similar way, predicament thinking embraces systems theory (El-Taliawi and Hartley, 2020; Checkland, 1989) and has the potential to shape policy framing around the idea that systemic disruptions are nonlinear, largely unmanageable, and growing deeper and more consequential over time. These disruptions render existing norms of policymaking and implementation irrelevant and anachronistic, as the assumption of predictable, stable, and static contexts recalls the willfully naïve myopia of rationalism (Hartley et al, 2019). By significantly altering the once comfortably predictable context of problem framing, systemic disruptions compel policymakers not merely to optimize and update existing policy tools but also to critically revisit conceptualizations about the role, legitimacy, and purpose of policy itself.

Systemic oscillation of the sort generated by wicked problems like climate change has implications for the logical core of policy. Instead of operating within fixed, stable, and linear concepts of risk and risk management, policy in a disruptive, nonlinear era is compelled to embrace a new vocabulary better suited for understanding systemic collapse, disruption, and liminality (Kuecker and Hartley, 2020). This new vocabulary would reflect such uncertainties by embracing a revised understanding of social constructs (e.g., society, politics, economics, and culture) and their complex and often tenuous interdependencies. The vocabulary would also have the epistemic power to transform how knowledge is constituted and the terms on which it is contested. Such a dramatic paradigm shift would reconceptualize policymaking in ways that scarcely resemble current notions like problem definition, measurement, and resolution. The new system would enable the emergence of new ideas or, in a softer revolutionary process, a reanimation of current ideas with stronger social, political, and epistemic legitimacy; the pathways of the revolution are impossible to map, but the potential of an epistemic revolution is a liminal state contingency that policymakers and scholars cannot ignore. The unpredictability with which this revolution could materialize prevents us from making specific declarations about what new policy logics would look like. However, the point of this argument concerns primarily the shift itself: that is, the disruption to existing ways of thinking and the realignment of power and privilege during and after a period of epistemic liminality. Remaining flexible, resourceful, and open minded is the only way policymakers can assume the posture needed for this epistemic shift.

Predicament thinking could be inadvertently hampered or actively resisted by the systems and acolytes of legacy thinking. Indeed, a soft collapse generates a fog of epistemic transition that undercuts the hegemony of rationalism and even that of its replacement candidates. Like social change makers in the era of twentieth-century progressivism, advocates of a new paradigm may need to frame progress in long-term arcs and anticipate an incremental "one-step forward, two-steps back" process of change. Breaking from the old paradigms may also engender a sociocultural dissonance resulting from political opportunism and populist backlash, as evident in the 36 percent of US adults and 56 percent of self-identified Republicans who in early 2019 opposed policy measures to reduce the use of fossil fuels as a means to mitigate climate change (McCarthy, 2019). The tenuous survival of old epistemics even in reshaped form, and the disruption caused by emergent epistemics, may also further cleave practice from scholarship; policymakers could persist in their technocratic search for solutions with only marginal adjustments to process dimensions, finding scant applied value in the revolutionarily epistemics discussed by critical scholars.

Future research should develop mechanics of predicament thinking that require an anticipatory orientation, while recognizing that current best practice approaches to wicked problems merely perpetuate a flawed epistemic that often focuses predominantly on better ways of doing the wrong things. While policy agendas such as the SDGs and UN Habitat's New Urban Agenda adopt time frames in the 10-to-20-year range, the policy field must consider anticipatory time horizons that extend from 30 to 50, and even 100 years or more into the future. The exigencies of ecosystem disruption ask for foresight but in turn confound that foresight by being difficult to model, beset by wide confidence intervals, and susceptible to unanticipated change. Predicament thinking calls on policymakers to embrace nonlinearity in foresight processes despite the field's resolutely linear propensities. Furthermore, rationalist policy thinking is limited often by the truncated time horizons of capitalist logic and short-term economic gain (as fiscal ambitions and political selling points); such thinking is therefore appropriate for addressing only those few problems with similar horizons. Policy informed by such thinking may prove to be catastrophically anachronistic in the long arc of history due to its inability to see beyond the nonlinear horizon, which ecologists understand to be the planetary system's time scale. Further research is needed to explore whether and how a significant property of the predicament-based paradigm shift should be an adjustment to time horizons – an orientation requiring the decisive and unconditional abandonment of linearity in exchange for nonlinearity or circularity. The research agenda concerning predicament thinking thus requires fundamental shifts in how scholarship valorizes and perpetuates existing epistemics (even in ostensible service to new thinking), how it conceptualizes disciplines and their connections, and how it regards and presents certitude in its own claims.

4.4 Insights about Transition from Policy Change Theory

This section concludes Section 4 by situating the preceding discussion of three modes of policy thinking within existing theories about policy change to explain how academic understandings of policy change help identify what might emerge from public policy's liminal state. The overlap with policy change illustrates how these two theoretical worlds might merge, while providing actionable guidance as policy change can be seen as characteristic of a soft collapse and epistemic liminality. Policy change for this purpose refers to a generic change in the content, instrument choice, and settings or calibrations of existing policies or the introduction of new policies or elements of policy; it can refer also to the redesign of systems for policymaking, as broadly conceptualized by theories of the policy process (from agenda setting to evaluation; see Jann and Wegrich, 2007). This section provides a link between the preceding discussion about epistemic transition and the more practical mechanics of how policy systems as understood by policy change theory might shape or reinterpret epistemic transition. In so doing, this section examines three canonical frameworks included in Orach and Schlüter's 2016 examination of how policy change frameworks are applied to environmental issues: Kingdon and Thurber's (1984) multiple streams, Jenkins-Smith and Sabatier's (1993) advocacy coalition, and Baumgartner and Jones's (1993) punctuated equilibrium. These three are selected for their collective representation of mainstream scholarly thinking about policy change; others, such as Ostrom's institutional analysis and development (IAD) framework and social-ecological systems (SES) framework, are equilibrium-based perspectives that explain the institutional contexts around why policies or resource management systems have settled into a steady state –

sustainable or otherwise. Network-based theories (Adam and Kriesi, 2007) and innovation and diffusion theories (Berry and Berry, 2007) of policy change are relevant to particular types of policy dynamics but do not fit as well with our argument about epistemic transformation due to their bounded analytical frames. We acknowledge that future research may endeavor to interpret our argument about epistemic transition within any of these omitted theories and frameworks.

These three frameworks are included not because they claim to provide solutions to policy problems but because, in explaining policy change, they relate directly to problem conceptualization. We argue that these largely rationalist theories are adaptable enough to accommodate shifts in the epistemology of problem framing, and that without such accommodation they and others would offer only an incomplete picture of the policy mandate characterizing the convergence of systemic crises. Rationalist policy's epistemic core assumes, as do most policy epistemics, its own objectivity and common sense – rendering it a stable and politically valid, if static, tool for pursuing solutions. Understanding how the radically shifting contexts of a global system in the liminal state of soft collapse alter the meta-structures of policy, and how these shifts also alter the conceptual and practical relationships among power, agency, and governance, brings a fresh perspective that creates space for the refinement of long accepted theories of policy change.

We provide a minimally descriptive background for each framework, as detailed explanations are beyond the scope of this Element but can be accessed in the referenced literature. This comparative analysis aims to be systematic while remaining at a high enough level to derive broadly applicable insights. We then overlay the three previously introduced modes of thinking (technocratic, Frankfurt, and predicament) with the three frameworks (multiple streams, advocacy coalition, and punctuated equilibrium). We further enrich the analysis through the three subdimensions of comparison utilized by Schlager's (1999) comparison of the same frameworks: model of the individual, collective action, and institutions. We select these dimensions because they respectively account for micro (individual), meso (group), and macro (system) variables. To facilitate the analysis, each of these dimensions is reduced to a simple operationalizable concept (italicized in parentheses in Table 2, which summarizes the results of this exercise). We intend the framework to illustrate how dominant understandings about the basic building blocks of public policy (i.e., individuals, groups and collective action, and contexts as institutions) are reinterpreted across various plausible modes of thinking, exhibiting how the relevance of some epistemic constructs may survive liminality while other constructs are ripe for dismissal based on their service to anachronistic thinking.

Table 2 Comparison of policy change frameworks across modes of thinking

		Technocratic thinking	Frankfurt thinking	Predicament thinking
Multiple streams	Model of the individual (*rational satisficer*)	Rational within empirical limits	Rational within bounds of knowledge type	Rational within evolving circumstances
	Collective action (*convergence of crisis drivers*)	Convergence defined by data patterns	Convergence dependent on knowledge type	Convergence recognized collectively
	Institutions (*politics-policy-problem interface*)	Circumvention of political process to align policy with problem	Contested understandings of crises under same policy capabilities	Alignment of political will with policy capability
Advocacy coalition	Model of the individual (*faithful to belief system*)	Faithful through protective information filters	Faithful according to knowledge types	Faithful amid narratives of change
	Collective action (*coordination of like interests*)	Coordination losing relevance	Coordination within epistemic silos	Coordination without clear understanding
	Institutions (*policy subsystems*)	Contested use of data and evidence along ideological lines	Marginalization of non-mainstream crisis definitions	Political splintering along crisis definition

Punctuated equilibrium			
Model of the individual (*steadfast to fixed preferences*)	Steadfast until enough contradictory information emerges	Steadfast according to knowledge types	Steadfast until abrupt disruptive change
Collective action (*contestation over event significance*)	Empirical	Epistemic	Political
Institutions (*venue shopping*)	Receptivity of venues to data and evidence	Venues siloed according to knowledge type	Elevating crisis urgency from local to national

The multiple streams framework theorizes that policy change occurs at the convergence of three dynamics metaphorically conceptualized as streams: problem, policy, and politics. The nexus of the convergence – conceptualized by the clashing metaphor of a policy window – is exploited by a policy entrepreneur with the motivation, capabilities, and political capital to marshal resources and support for affecting policy change. The model is further theorized by Zahariadis (2007) as occurring across two stages: a problem-policy-politics stage and a process-policy-politics stage, with the former describing agenda formation and the latter policy formulation and settlement. Howlett et al. (2015) add a program stream to the second stage to articulate "the specific instruments that would be used to realise the policy aims" (p. 428). Despite the discreditation of rational choice theory (Sen, 1977), particularly by scholarship about wicked problems and other knowledges, the multiple streams framework's model of the individual (not including the policy entrepreneur) can be described as that of a rational satisficer – that is, an individual seeking to maximize benefit and minimize cost given constraints on knowledge and resources. Collective action can be operationalized as collective understanding – for example, about drivers of global crises as conceptualized through individual streams of the framework. Institutions are operationalized as the policy context in which streams converge and generate a policy window.

The advocacy coalition framework focuses on the policymaking context as constitutive of subsystems and of the role and behavior of belief coalitions, variables that generate "a superior understanding of the conflict inherent within policy-making" (Howlett et al., 2017b, p. 69). Notable is the prospect that coalitions with differing belief systems come together to advance an issue-specific policy agenda that serves mutual interests. As it did for the multiple streams framework, this analytical exercise utilizes Schlager's three dimensions to deepen the comparison of modes of thinking on issues that relate specifically to our argument: model of the individual as faithful to a belief system, collective action as the coordination of interests around a belief-based policy agenda or initiative, and institutions as constitutive of policy subsystems in which the work of brokering, resource deployment, and strategic execution occur. Given the difference in focus between the multiple streams (opportunity moments) and advocacy coalition (collaborative dynamics) frameworks, policy implications across the three modes of thinking do not necessarily have parallel characteristics; the multiple streams framework focuses on convergence of enabling conditions while the advocacy coalition framework focuses on agency and actor behavior. Both perspectives have useful implications for studies of policymaking and policy capacity (for an application of policy capacity theories to the practical challenges of governance amid wicked problems and systemic disruption, see Hartley et al., 2019).

Finally, punctuated equilibrium theory examines policy as a stable phenomenon perpetuated by policy monopolists but occasionally and abruptly interrupted by endogenous or exogenous change (e.g., global crises). The theory largely assumes that policies exist in equilibrium until the occurrence of a shock event or short period of significant change, which in turn generates a new policy equilibrium in a progression that over time resembles a step function or incremental process. For the analysis of punctuated equilibrium theory, this exercise applies the three Schlager dimensions as it did for the other two frameworks. The model of the individual is one who is faithful to a set of policy preferences that are fixed and thus stabilize the policy environment. Collective action occurs not as a driver of policy change but as an image shaper for a new policy context or new set of policy circumstances, with competition over narratives that define the change and its outcomes. Institutions are interpreted in the context of venue shopping, reflecting the complexities of policy stability and change within – for example – the type of multi-level governance environments characterizing federal or quasi-federal systems. As with the other frameworks, policy implications are outlined Table 2 in a way that reflects the exigencies of systemic disruption and global crises as treated by the three modes of thinking.

Our discussion posits that public policy's emerging epistemic foundations are shaped in practical application by the combined insights of technocratic, Frankfurt, and predicament thinking as read through the three policy change frameworks outlined earlier. Technocratic thinking brings a deterministic calm to multiple streams-based scenarios by delimiting the bounds of rationalism through the empirics of big data and analytics, providing quantifiable evidence of the convergence of policy change streams and aligning the problem with clearly articulated governance capacities. This scenario reduces the messy political contestation around defining stream characteristics but is subject to political pushback (as seen in populist movements challenging expert authority and technocracy) and the hidden bias nested within the design and function of data processing systems. Frankfurt thinking brings a tone of epistemic contestation to the multiple streams framework, with rationalism shaped only by perception and conceptualization of policy streams and negotiated based on the determinations of epistemic models and competing knowledges (e.g., Enlightenment, indigenous, Confucian, feminist, and queer, among others). Even policy capabilities can elude consensus understanding, as Klein (2015) illustrates, with the power of policy entrepreneurs neutralized in an environment of shifting definitions, contexts, and truth claims. This scenario has a fatalistic undertone of seemingly irreconcilable difference, testing the practical limits of democratic governance processes at various stages of the policy process (Benegal and Scruggs, 2018). For the multiple streams framework, predicament thinking assumes a flexible collective rationalism amid the convergence of factors that elevate the visibility of ecosystem collapse as a policy urgency. Under predicament thinking, policy change is not necessarily a solution to a well-defined problem but a strategy for managing intractable and persistent challenges visited by ecosystem crises. Policy change is leveraged, or attempted so, by a policy entrepreneur such as an individual (e.g., Greta Thunberg), organization (e.g., the UN), ideology (e.g., Western political liberalism, neo-liberalism), or social movement (e.g., environmental justice).

The advocacy coalition framework offers an altogether different account of how policy might change across modes of thinking. With its focus on interest group alignment, the framework is particularly relevant in the current environment of political contestation; the modeled individual is faithful to a belief system but can build a coalition to advance a policy agenda shared across differing belief systems. Coordination of actors within policy subsystems, however, is no guarantee that non-mainstream definitions of what constitutes a crisis avoid marginalization by hegemonic actors. The framework underscores the liminality and uncertainty of predicament thinking, wherein the interest group ecosystem further fractures while certitude about policy effectiveness erodes with the introduction of new information or new framing of existing information. Furthermore, new coalitions can form along a fault line demarcating two views of policy: one as a solution to root causes of manageable problems and the other as a means to mitigate negative impacts of intractable problems. Similar fault lines could emerge within conceptual-technocratic thinking between empiricists and constructivists or within technical-technocratic thinking between techno-futurists and luddites.

Punctuated equilibrium theory provides a means to explain the dynamics around a shock event impacting the policy status quo or incremental trajectory. Although ecosystem crises like climate change are typically characterized as a slowly evolving phenomenon relative to time frames experienced by human society, outlier climate events with extreme impacts have the potential to command policy attention in a phenomenon called a focusing event (Birkland, 1998). After such an event (e.g., the 2020 Australia wildfires and the 2019 heat wave in Europe), political contestation emerges around the event's ontological characterization and significance or urgency for policy intervention. In the context of predicament thinking, a given event's significance is politically negotiated in epistemically familiar ways; debates about its impact severity and likely recurrence focus on determining appropriate policy solutions. Advocates failing to gain political purchase for stronger or longer-term intervention can venue shop for a sympathetic policy audience among legal jurisdictions, global epistemic communities, and other arenas. Klein (2015) argues that debates about climate change denial, attribution, severity, or resolution are further ignited after severe weather events. Contestation about the significance of shock events as destabilizers of equilibrium is an epistemic issue under Frankfurt thinking and an empirical issue under technocratic thinking; the former concerns debates about the nature of knowledge, while the latter concerns debates about the reliability of scientific data. Furthermore, policy instabilities caused by the impact of shock events can jump sectoral boundaries. For example, discussions about the difficulty of addressing a climate change shock event have boundary jumped into discussions about financing climate change adaptation; boundaries were again crossed when these discussions merged into other discussions about assigning responsibility for the crisis and the associated obligations to carry the financial burden. Similar dynamics were apparent during the COVID-19 pandemic, as a public health problem became an economic problem and, ultimately in some countries, a political problem related to declarations about the urgency of the pandemic and the degree of economic sacrifice appropriate in undertaking containment and mitigation measures.

In reflecting more broadly on the analytical exercise in Table 2, there are some limitations with implications for future research. First, the most significant limitation is conceptual overlap among the studied modes of thinking; they are neither mutually exclusive nor collectively exhaustive. Elements of technocratic thinking are present in predicament thinking, as the latter's effort to manage impacts rather than directly confronting definable problems can involve technology and rationalist thinking as tools for analysis, implementation, and other tasks in the policymaking process. There is also no definitional reason why predicament thinking should avoid consideration of alternative knowledges as suggested by Frankfurt thinking. Second, regarding policy change frameworks, shock events assumed to occur in punctuated equilibrium theory can play a role in both the multiple streams framework (as the immediate emergence or realization of a problem stream) and the advocacy coalition framework (as an event that generates a rallying point for multiple interest groups). Finally, advocacy coalitions as interest groups can be actors in the other two frameworks, entrepreneurially advancing policy change within a policy window in the multiple streams framework or attempting to monopolize the narrative about the significance of a shock event in punctuated equilibrium theory.

Despite these overlaps, this exercise is useful in specifying how elements of each mode of thinking or policy change framework overlaps with others and generates a set of variables for case analysis (as stated by Ostrom [2011] to be one purpose of a framework). The exercise further seeks to capture the social dynamics of defining problems, extending the ideas of Conklin (2006) on the relationship between cultural conditions, collective intelligence, wicked problems, and the fragmentation of "perspectives, understandings, and intentions of the collaborators" (p. 1) that confounds the problem definition and problem-solving processes. The exercise also captures three roles shaping problem framing and narrative building: that of the individual, the group or society, and the institutions that shape the behaviors of both. We argue that discussions about environmental policy in a time of instability and transition occur largely within one of these three modes of thinking and not across them, justifying the analysis of each separately in the context of epistemic transition and of departures from the rationalist performance of policymaking. The theoretical usefulness is the examination of these modes through the lenses of three canonical frameworks of policy change, in an effort to reveal fresh theoretical perspectives on how the convergence of systemic crises characterizing the twenty-first century and their subsequent liminal state of systemic transition can be problematized and addressed.

We conclude Section 4 by outlining opportunities for additional research. First, the comparison of how policy, as analyzed through three common policy change frameworks, might epistemically treat global crises in the age of epistemic liminality, transition, and political disruption, can be applied to case studies and quantitative longitudinal or panel-based studies. Cases can be screened based on the presence of policy change as a natural experimental treatment, enabling an understanding of before- and after-treatment contexts across factors like epistemic bias, organizational cultures, and sociopolitical forces. Research designs can include a comparison of how multiple frameworks treat the same case or how two cases are treated by the same framework. Such research can contribute to practical understandings about policymaking under predicament circumstances and the liminal state of soft collapse and can contribute to theoretical revivals of and amendments to policy change frameworks that have already seen one generation of application and refinement. Second, the three modes of thinking can provide further richness to case analyses by mobilizing alternative literatures that cross-cut theoretical silos within policy scholarship. Such work has practical relevance in identifying which policy practices surface under given predicament conditions and how organizational, institutional, and systemic contexts hinder or facilitate such practices.

5 Conclusion

The old ways of thinking and doing have led the world to a soft collapse and arguably cannot be counted on to deliver a transformative change of course. We have argued in this Element that the twenty-first century will be characterized by the convergence of multiple wicked problems that approach an existential threshold where society becomes more vulnerable to shock events. COVID-19 is both an example of such a shock event and a time-condensed illustration of how the longer unfolding impacts of systemic crises can destabilize the truth claims on which the legitimacy of policy and governance are built. This phenomenon suggests a looming period of epistemic liminality that forces the policy field into a profound reckoning about how it understands itself and its role in society. Under such circumstances, opportunities for research-driven theoretical advancement become more apparent; to this end, we have explored the applicability of formative concepts in the policy sciences – including the intelligence function – to understanding epistemic hegemony. To map a possible agenda for future research in policy theory, we then overlaid legacy theories of policy change over three proposed modes of thinking that represent different and sometimes competing epistemics. Ultimately, we conclude that ways of thinking about and doing public policy – along with policies themselves – that emerge from the fog of epistemic liminality are unknowable, and that the policy field must be prepared to divest itself from its own anachronistic thinking to remain receptive and relevant in the process of emergence that likely lies ahead.

The salience of the climate crisis, as a rallying point for international cooperation via institutions like the UN and initiatives like the SDGs, invites scrutiny about how policy problems are understood. Naming and framing such problems, a privilege typically enjoyed by the economic and political elite, is a starting point for such scrutiny. However, understanding decades of policy failures and limited successes addressing wicked problems and the dim prospects of anachronistic policy approaches to address them any more effectively in the future mandates research that takes a deeper critical dive into the path dependency of policymaking epistemics. We have argued in this Element that the pandemic-driven soft collapse's liminal state is an occasion to visit the epistemological underpinnings of public policy itself. This Element has thus called for a related research agenda and has illustrated how such an agenda might be structured around existing policy theories in a way that allows new modes of thinking to emerge from the liminal state and reshape or wholly supplant them. We have argued that public policy will struggle to endure the twin forces of epistemic instability and the ecologically induced transition problem, and that neither the more committed application of technology and technocratic thinking nor minor tweaks to the design and function of policies and policymaking systems are sufficient to overcome a deficit of collective understanding about systemic crises or the capacity for epistemic self-reflection.

The epistemic foundations of Enlightenment rationalism are implicated in the modern sustainability policy predicament, and with the rise of populist and post-truth rhetoric in the political discourse, small cracks in the legitimacy of policy systems are becoming more visible (Lockie, 2017; Suiter, 2016). As truth claims falter amid the declining credibility of elite expertise, post-truth (or post-empiricist) movements could render modern policy constructs antiquated and anachronistic. Donald Trump's efforts to discredit public health officials and foment anti-mask sentiment during the COVID-19 pandemic, along with his campaign to sow doubt in the legitimacy of the 2020 presidential election outcome (culminating in the US Capitol building invasion during the counting of electoral college votes), illustrate the power and danger of post-truth politics. Policy thus faces the predicament of reclaiming its legitimacy, at a time when it desperately needs that legitimacy. As society enters into a period of soft collapse–induced epistemic liminality, no single way of thinking dominates and the void becomes a hotly contested space – this leads to a fog of transition and potential dark age for a governance style that once thrived on epistemic coherence, uniformity, and certitude. Research that explores the cavernous theoretical reaches of this argument has the potential to liberate policy from the strictures of anachronistic thinking and contributes to the emergence of a new way of thinking about policymaking and policy theory.

Science and evidence are commonly seen as the epistemic building blocks of rationalist policymaking. Accordingly, the Lasswellian policy scientist of democracy embodies the romanticized image of a professional moving between scientific and political realms. In addressing the climate crisis, the work of natural scientists provides a case for immediate and transformational policy action. Despite such scientific admonitions, however, policy action remains highly contested politically – in some cases to the point of stalemate. Interpreting this phenomenon in the context of efforts to undermine democratic institutions, as seen not only in one-party states but also in long-time democracies, reveals research opportunities to revisit the intersection of politics, epistemic transition, and existential threats to humanity. According to Farr et al. (2008), the world is threatened by "ignorance, force, and totalitarian ideologies" (p. 22). When these ideological pathologies converge with, rather than diverge from, the intelligence function, the epistemic waters get muddier. This process is complicated more broadly by what Klein (2015) argues is the threat to capitalism posed by climate change and efforts by those with a deep stake in capitalist reproduction to conceal truth about climate change and undermine the intelligence function.

The lingering question for scholarship is whether Lasswell's ideas can be used to re-politicize or re-humanize a deepening policy epistemic – on sustainability in particular – that makes overtures to other knowledges but remains problem defined by only what it can see and measure (Hartley, 2020). Indeed, the climate policy scientist of democracy may be the echoes of Lasswell's voice in an era when aspects of old ideas worth keeping still beg for revisitation and novel interpretation. The contradictory and incomplete nature of Lasswell's concept leaves it open to interpretation and is perhaps its best chance for new relevance amid epistemic liminality and contradictions among science, political values, and other knowledges. According to Farr et al. (2006), the policy scientist of democracy was "at once positivist and value-laden, elitist and democratic, heroic and implausible" (p. 579), exhibiting a heroism and quietism that are "always in creative tension" (p. 586); the policy scientist of democracy is "a scholar divided against himself" (p. 583). If the policy scientist of democracy is to gain new currency in original or altered form, contextual and analytical factors will also need a rethink. Farr et al. (2008) argue that Laswell harbored an enthusiasm for "government planning and autonomous expert leadership" (p. 586). This idea casts science and democracy into stark relief; without a way to epistemologically harmonize them, coexistence and mutual trust between them are the only ways policy practice may find the concept useful in an era of epistemic liminality and thereafter.

The current implication, perhaps not as Lasswell envisioned at the time, of the policy scientist of democracy is that scholarship and practice should engage with other knowledges in a way that avoids co-optation but recognizes their value as equal to that of empiricist and rationalist knowledge. It is debatable, however, whether rationalism is capable of the epistemic flexibility needed for such a compromise. The future of anachronistic epistemics is dependent not on their doubling-down but on their humility and willingness to see their own limitations while recognizing the validity of rival perspectives. Indeed, this lingering tension is exhibited in the modern political arena. In an increasingly contested and disruptive political context, trust in institutions and governance is declining in Western democracies and around the world more generally (Krastev, 2019; van Beek et al., 2019). However, even the structures underlying trust as a social construct (including truth) face disruption and render trust itself highly unstable. McDougal et al. (1973) provided a pithy summary of associated challenges: "the reduction of intelligence to a patent base of political power politicizes every participant in the intelligence process" (p. 426). The scientists and policymakers of democracy (or otherwise) must face a late-stage rationalism in which the legitimacy of commonsense policy narratives is under stress. The tools of natural and social sciences – technologies, scholarly concepts, and analytical models – may attempt to evolve and provide deeper insights into the contexts and characteristics of wicked policy problems and coming systemic crises, but will the political feasibility of associated policy measures follow suit?

A policy science improved within existing epistemic frames may be seen as a sunrise moment for particular types of problems but can also widen the gap between technocratic authority and the governed. Forcing technocracy to reflect on its own epistemic foundations are the presence of other knowledges, whimsical populist mandates that declare high confidence in their own legitimacy, and AI as an entity with agency in both knowledge generation and policy-making. Just as crucial is what happens when the moment of epistemic liminality unfolds; to what degree is anachronistic public policy capable of changing and absorbing alternative ideas? According to the IPCC,[11] "education, information, and community approaches, including those that are informed by indigenous knowledge and local knowledge, can accelerate the wide-scale behaviour changes consistent with adapting to and limiting global warming." As a language of inquiry, science is fundamentally rooted in social and political systems that extend beyond the elite technocratic communities where public policy is often made.

A twenty-first-century policy scientist of democracy recognizes that empirical certitude, while the product of science and technological progress, is weak tea for the proverbial angry mob and a poor substitute for the richness of other knowledges. Even the act of analyzing the phenomenon of epistemic contestation, as undertaken in this Element, eludes full social scientific understanding and compels us to adopt some speculative propositions. The research pathways we have articulated are not merely a scholarly parlor game but an urgent imperative for humanity – particularly in a world where political pushback is coalescing around the idea that the public has had, in the words of British politician Michael Andrew Gove, "enough of experts" (cited in Clarke and Newman, 2017). At the same time, the possible convergence of technocracy and populism (see Bickerton and Accetti [2021] concerning "techno-populism") suggests that there may be some political purpose and residual utility in instrumental rationalism – even in democratic contexts. This depends, however, on epistemological factors concerning the construction of truth, namely the claims to legitimacy made by expertise as against "popular" wisdom. Where either is able to convincingly use the other to strengthen its claims, both technocracy and populism may be seen as two sides of the same coin – one that represents a seeming alternative to long-entrenched institutions like party politics. A question for further contemplation is whether technocracy and populism, as they exist concurrently, provide a counterbalance to each other

---

[11] www.ipcc.ch/sr15/chapter/spm/

that prevents the broader political-ideological system from tipping too far in one direction. Can such seemingly opposite forces, one the legitimacy of expertise and the other of popular wisdom, coexist productively or are they doomed to confrontation? Our argument would suggest that technocracy is under greater political and existential threat due to the anachronism of its intellectual legacy. At the same time, we do not see populism as the inevitably victorious epistemic that emerges from liminality but as an ideologically vacuous reaction to politically manufactured perceptions of threats. If both survive the fog of epistemic transition, they may share space with ways of thinking that are new or currently undiscovered. This post-liminal state would mark an intellectual and existential moment as profound as the Enlightenment and should be embraced as an opportunity for fundamental reform in policy practice and scholarship.

In interrogating the fate of fact and politics in twenty-first century politics, it is crucial to critically reflect not only on the policy sciences but also the social sciences more generally – and, at the highest level of abstraction, Enlightenment thinking and its cultural ubiquity. We have argued that Enlightenment thinking is the intellectual provenance of the twentieth-century rationalist project that remains embedded in modern thinking about social sciences and public policy specifically. At the same time, we recognize that our position can be critiqued for its uncertainty about the future. In response, we conclude with some prescriptive reflections about a path forward. First, public policy must shift from solutionism to predicament thinking, including research approaches that embrace and enhance ideas about emergence and policy practitioners who embrace the normative, value-informed, and self-empowering aspects of their profession. Connolly's work on a "world becoming" (2011) leads him to advocate for democratic activism (2013) – an idea we support but not without the cautionary insistence that scholars and practitioners dismantle vertical relations of power from their epistemic roots. Second, public policy's long-standing ideological and institutional fusion with capitalism should be radically reimagined in deference to alternative and emerging models like bioregionalism and economic and productive circularity. Further, anti-oppression frameworks like critical race theory, feminist and queer theories, and crip theory represent foundational premises for new policy approaches. Indeed, the liminal state's policy of emergence should decolonize (Tuck and Yang, 2012) in ways that not only recognize the historical injustices of settler colonialism but also extend beyond the politics of apology to engage reconciliation and reparation as pathways to accountability for policy's sins of commission and omission. That such ideas lack immediate practical feasibility is no excuse to dismiss them as utopian pipe dreams. To become relevant in the liminal state and overcome its anachronistic epistemic, policy should embrace ideas like

Levitas's (2013) "utopia as method." As much as there are calls for a new epistemology targeting wicked problems, and as much as the prospect of convergent crises and systemic collapse mandate such an epistemology, so too is it time for radical pedagogies and scholarship to critically interrogate modernity's faith in anachronistic policy logics and to make space for whatever is next. The liminal state and end of modernity liberate such possibilities and signal a restarting of history.

References

Ackoff, R. L. (2010). *Differences That Make a Difference: An Annotated Glossary of Distinctions Important in Management.* Axminster, UK: Triarchy Press Limited.

Adam, S., and Kriesi H. (2007). The network approach. In Sabatier, P., ed., *Theories of Public Policy.* Bolder, CO: Westview Press, pp. 129–149.

Adorno, T., and Horkheimer, M. (2002 [1945]). In Noerr, G. S., ed. Jephcott, E., trans. *Dialectic of Enlightenment: Philosophical Fragments.* Stanford, CA: Stanford University Press.

Agrawal, A., and Bauer, J. (2005). *Environmentality: Technologies of Government and the Making of Subjects.* Durham, NC: Duke University Press.

Aldy, J. E., Barrett, S., and Stavins, R. N. (2003). Thirteen plus one: A comparison of global climate policy architectures. *Climate Policy*, 3(4), 373–397.

Aldy, J. E., Pizer, W. A., and Akimoto, K. (2017). Comparing emissions mitigation efforts across countries. *Climate Policy*, 17(4), 501–515.

Alexander, J. C. (2013). *The Dark Side of Modernity.* Malden, MA: Polity Press.

Anheier, H. K. (2019a). On the future of the public policy school. *Global Policy*, 10(1), 75–83.

Anheier, H. K. (2019b). Towards the new Lasswell school of public policy. *Global Policy*, 10(1), 104–106.

Anthem, P. (2020). Risk of hunger pandemic as COVID-19 set to almost double acute hunger by end of 2020. *World Food Program Insight*, April 16. https://insight.wfp.org/covid-19-will-almost-double-people-in-acute-hunger-by-end-of-2020-59df0c4a8072

Arato, A., and Gebhardt, E. (Eds.). (1978). *The Essential Frankfurt School Reader.* Oxford: Blackwell.

Arendt, H. (1958). *The Human Condition.* Chicago: University of Chicago Press.

Arnstein, S. R. (1969). A ladder of citizen participation. *Journal of the American Institute of Planners*, 35(4), 216–224.

Ascher, W. (2007). Policy sciences contributions to analysis to promote sustainability. *Sustainability Science*, 2(2), 141–149.

Ascher, W. (1987). Policy sciences and the economic approach in a "post-positivist" era. *Policy Sciences*, 20(1), 3–9.

Barth, F. (1995). Other knowledge and other ways of knowing. *Journal of Anthropological Research*, 51(1), 65–68.

Barth, T. J., and Arnold, E. (1999). Artificial intelligence and administrative discretion: Implications for public administration. *The American Review of Public Administration*, 29(4), 332–351.

Baumgartner, F., and Jones, B. (1993). *Agendas and Instability in American Politics*. Chicago: University of Chicago Press.

Bazaz, A., Paolo B., Buckeridge, M., Cartwright, A., de Coninck, H., Engelbrecht, D. et al. (2018). "Summary for Urban Policymakers – What the IPCC Special Report on 1.5C Means for Cities." Indian Institute for Human Settlements, Bangalore, India. http://doi.org/10.24943/SCPM.2018

Benegal, S., and Scruggs, L. (2018). Correcting misinformation about climate change: The impact of partisanship in an experimental setting. *Climatic Change*, 148(2), 61–80.

Benjamin, R. (2019). Race after technology: Abolitionist tools for the new Jim code. *Social Forces*, 98(4), 1–3.

Bennett, N., and Lemoine, J. (2014). What VUCA really means for you. *Harvard Business Review*, 92(1), 10.

Berger, T., and Esguerra, A. (Eds.). (2017). *World Politics in Translation: Power, Relationality and Difference in Global Cooperation*. New York: Routledge Press.

Bernauer, T., and Böhmelt, T. (2013). National climate policies in international comparison: The climate change cooperation index. *Environmental Science & Policy*, 25,196–206.

Berry, F., and Berry, D. (2007). Innovation and diffusion models in policy research. In Sabatier, P., ed. *Theories of the Policy Process*. Boulder, CO: Westview Press, pp. 253–297.

Best, S., and Kellner, D. (1997). *The Postmodern Turn*. New York: Guilford Press.

Bickerton, C. J., and Accetti, C. I. (2021). *Technopopulism: The New Logic of Democratic Politics*. Oxford: Oxford University Press.

Birkland, T. A. (1998). Focusing events, mobilization, and agenda setting. *Journal of Public Policy*, 18(1), 53–74.

Bruntland Commission. (1987). *Our Common Future: The World Commission on Environment and Development*. Oxford: Oxford University Press.

Burris, B. H. (1993). *Technocracy at Work*. Albany: State University of New York Press.

Byrne, D. S. (1998). *Complexity Theory and the Social Sciences: An Introduction*. New York: Routledge Press.

Cairney, P., Heikkila, T., and Wood, M. (2019). *Making Policy in a Complex World*. Cambridge: Cambridge University Press.

Caldwell, B. (2015). *Beyond Positivism*. New York: Routledge Press.

Checkland, P. B. (1989). Soft systems methodology. *Human Systems Management*, 8(4), 273–289.

Christian, B. (2020). *The Alignment Problem: Machine Learning and Human Values*. New York: W.W. Norton & Company.

Clarke, J., and Newman, J. (2017). "People in this country have had enough of experts": Brexit and the paradoxes of populism. *Critical Policy Studies*, 11(1), 101–116.

Clarke, J., Stubbs, P., Lendvai, N., and Bainton, D. (2015). *Making Policy Move: Towards a Politics of Translation and Assemblage*. Bristol, UK: Policy Press.

Cole, J. (2020). "A Toothpick in a Tsunami": US big oil faces bankruptcy as prices plunge 30% on Saudi expansion. *Informed Comment*, March 9, www .juancole.com/2020/03/toothpick-bankruptcy-expansion.html

Colebatch, H. K. (2018). The idea of policy design: Intention, process, outcome, meaning and validity. *Public Policy and Administration*, *33*(4), 365–383.

Conklin, J. (2006). *Wicked Problems and Social Complexity*. San Francisco, CA: CogNexus Institute.

Connolly, W. (2013). *The Fragility of Things: Self-Organizing Processes, Neoliberal Fantasies, and Democratic Activism*. Durham, NC: Duke University Press.

Connolly, W. (2011). A *World of Becoming*. Durham, NC: Duke University Press.

Cooke, B. (2001). "From Colonial Administration to Development Management." IDPM General Discussion Papers 63/2001, DOI: 10.22004/ ag.econ.30562

Cortés, U., Sànchez-Marrè, M., Ceccaroni, L., R-Roda, I., and Poch, M. (2000). Artificial intelligence and environmental decision support systems. *Applied Intelligence*, 13(1), 77–91.

Daly, H. E. (1991). *Steady-State Economics: With New Essays*. Washington, DC: Island Press.

Dawes, S. S. (2008). The evolution and continuing challenges of e-governance. *Public Administration Review*, 68,S86–S102.

Defries, R., and Nagendra, H. (2017). Ecosystem management as a wicked problem. *Science*, 356,265–270.

Delmas, M. A., and Burbano, V. C. (2011). The drivers of greenwashing. *California Management Review*, 54(1), 64–87.

Denhardt, R. B., and Denhardt, J. V. (2000). The new public service: Serving rather than steering. *Public Administration Review*, 60(6), 549–559.

De Roeck, F. (2019). Governmentality and the climate-development nexus: The case of the EU Global Climate Change Alliance. *Global Environmental Change*, 55,160–167.

Dewey, J. (1931). The development of American pragmatism. In Thayer, H. S., ed., (1989), *Pragmatism: The Classic Writings*. Indianapolis, IN: Hackett, pp. 23–40.

Dryzek, J. S. (1990). *Discursive Democracy: Politics, Policy, and Political Science*. Cambridge: Cambridge University Press.

Duit, A. (2016). Resilience thinking: Lessons for public administration. *Public Administration*, *94*(2), 364–380.

Dunlap, R. E., and McCright, A. M. (2011). Organized climate change denial. In Dryzek, J. S., Norgaard, R. B., and Schlosberg, D., eds., *The Oxford Handbook of Climate Change and Society*. Oxford : Oxford University Press, pp. 144–160.

Dunlop, C. A. (2013). Epistemic communities. In Howlett, M., Fritzen, S., Xun, W., and Araral, E., eds., *Routledge Handbook of Public Policy*. New York : Routledge, pp. 229–243.

Dunn, W. N. (2019). *Pragmatism and the Origins of the Policy Sciences*. Cambridge: Cambridge University Press.

Dunn, W. N. (2018a). Harold Lasswell and the study of public policy. *Oxford Research Encyclopedias*. Doi:10.1093/acrefore/9780190228637.013.600. Available from https://oxfordre.com/politics/view/10.1093/acrefore/9780190228637.001.0001/acrefore-9780190228637-e-600

Dunn, W. N. (2018b). "Stage" theories of the policy process. In Colebatch, H. K., and Hoppe, R., eds., *Handbook on Policy, Process and Governing*. Cheltenham, UK: Edward Elgar Publishing, pp. 112–130.

Dunn, W. N., and Holzner, B. (1988). Knowledge in society: Anatomy of an emergent field. *Knowledge in Society*, 1(1), 3.

Dupuis, J., and Biesbroek, R. (2013). Comparing apples and oranges: The dependent variable problem in comparing and evaluating climate change adaptation policies. *Global Environmental Change*, 23(6), 1476–1487.

Durose, C., and Richardson, L. (2015). *Designing Public Policy for Co-production: Theory, Practice and Change*. Bristol, UK: Policy Press.

du Sautoy, M. (2019). *The Creativity Code: Art and Innovation in the Age of AI*. Cambridge, MA: Belknap Press.

Edis, T. (2020). A Revolt Against Expertise: Pseudoscience, Right-Wing Populism, and Post-Truth Politics. *Disputatio*, 9(13), 1–29.

Elkins, J., and Norris, A. (Eds.). (2012). *Truth and Democracy*. Philadelphia: University of Pennsylvania Press.

Ellwood, J. L. (1981). "Graduate Education for Non-Academic Careers in the Public Policy Schools: A Look at the Competition." Typescript of paper presented at the September meeting of the American Political Science Association, New York.

El-Taliawi, O., and Hartley, K. (2020). The COVID-19 crisis and complexity: A soft systems approach. *Journal of Contingencies and Crisis Management*, 29(1), 104–107.

Escobar, A. (2011). *Encountering Development: The Making and Unmaking of the Third World*. Princeton, NJ: Princeton University Press.

Esteva, G., and Prakash, M. S. (1998). *Grassroots Postmodernism: Remaking the Soil of Cultures*. London: Zed Books, Ltd.

Estlund, D. (1993). Making truth safe for democracy. In Copp, D., Hampton, J., and Roemer, E., eds., *The Idea of Democracy*. Cambridge: Cambridge University Press, pp. 71–100.

Eubanks, V. (2018). *Automating Inequality: How High-Tech Tools Profile, Police, and Punish the Poor*. New York : St. Martin's Press.

Farr, J., Hacker, J. S., and Kazee, N. (2008). Revisiting Lasswell. *Policy Sciences*, 41(1), 21–32.

Farr, J., Hacker, J. S., and Kazee, N. (2006). The policy scientist of democracy: The discipline of Harold D. Lasswell. *American Political Science Review*, 100(4), 579–587.

Ferguson, J. (1994). *The Anti-Politics Machine: "Development," Depoliticization, and Bureaucratic Power in Lesotho*. Minneapolis: University of Minnesota Press.

Fischer, F. (2019). Knowledge politics and post-truth in climate denial: On the social construction of alternative facts. *Critical Policy Studies*, 13(2), 133–152.

Fischer, F., Torgerson, D., Durnová, A., and Orsini, M. (Eds.). (2015). *Handbook of Critical Policy Studies*. Cheltenham, UK: Edward Elgar Publishing.

Fisher, D. R., Waggle, J,. and Leifeld, P. (2012). Where does political polarization come from? Locating polarization within the US climate change debate. *American Behavioral Scientist*, 57(1), 70–92.

Foucault, M. (2007). *Security, Territory, Population: Lectures at the Collège de France, 1977–78*. Davidson, A., ed.; Burchell, G., trans. Basingstoke, UK: Palgrave MacMillan.

Foucault, M. (1988). *Michel Foucault: Politics, Philosophy, Culture. Interviews and Other Writings, 1977–1984*. Kritzman, L. D., ed. New York: Routledge, 1988.

Frederickson, H. G. (1980). *New Public Administration*. Tuscaloosa University of Alabama Press.

Freeman, R. (2012). Reverb: Policy making in wave form. *Environment and Planning A*, 44(1), 13–20.

Friedman, J. (2019). *Power without Knowledge: A Critique of Technocracy.* Oxford: Oxford University Press.

Friedman, L. S. (1991). Economists and public policy programs. *Journal of Policy Analysis and Management*, 10(2), 343–359.

Geiger, R. S. (2009). Does Habermas understand the internet? The algorithmic construction of the blogo/public sphere. *Gnovis. A Journal of Communication, Culture, and Technology*, 10(1), 1–29.

Geyer, R., and Cairney, P. (Eds.). (2015). *Handbook on Complexity and Public Policy.* Cheltenham, UK: Edward Elgar Publishing.

Gore, A. (1992). *Earth in the Balance: Ecology and the Human Spirit.* New York: Houghton Mifflin Company.

Grundmann, R. (2017). The problem of expertise in knowledge societies. *Minerva*, 55(1), 25–48.

Haas, P. (1992). Epistemic communities and international policy coordination. *International Organization*, 46,1–35.

Hale, C. (2004). Rethinking indigenous politics in the era of the "Indio Permitido." *NACLA: Report on the Americas*, (September/October), pp. 16–21.

Hall, P. A., and Taylor, R. C. (1996). Political science and the three new institutionalisms. *Political Studies*, 44(5), 936–957.

Harari, Y. N. (2018). *21 Lessons for the Twenty-first Century.* New York: Spiegel & Grau.

Hartley, K. (2020). The epistemics of policymaking: From technocracy to critical pragmatism in the UN Sustainable Development Goals. *International Review of Public Policy*, 2(2), 233–244.

Hartley, K., and Ahmad, N. (2019). "Neo-professionalization of the Public Service: Opportunity or Threat for Policy Sciences Education?" First Workshop on the Future of Policy Sciences, sponsored by the Department of Asian and Policy Studies, the Education University of Hong Kong.

Hartley, K., and Kuecker, G. D. (2020). The moral hazards of smart water management. *Water International*, 45(6), 693–701.

Hartley, K., Kuecker, G. D., and Woo, J. J. (2019). Practicing public policy in an age of disruption. *Policy Design and Practice*, 2(2), 163–181.

Hartley, K., and Vu, M. K. (2020). Fighting fake news in the COVID-19 era: Policy insights from an equilibrium model. *Policy Sciences*, 53(4), 735–758.

Head, B. W. (2019). Forty years of wicked problems literature: Forging closer links to policy studies. *Policy and Society*, 38(2), 180–197.

Heclo, H. (1978). Issue networks and the executive establishment. In King, A., ed., *The New American Political System*. Washington, DC: American Enterprise Institute, pp. 87–104.

Heng, M. S., and De Moor, A. (2003). From Habermas's communicative theory to practice on the internet. *Information Systems Journal*, 13(4), 331–352.

Hershock, P. D. (2006). *Buddhism in the Public Sphere: Reorienting Global Interdependence*. New York : Routledge Press.

Hessels, L. K., Franssen, T., Scholten, W., & de Rijcke, S. (2019). Variation in valuation: How research groups accumulate credibility in four epistemic cultures. *Minerva*, 57(2), 127–149.

Hickman, L. A., and Alexander, T. M. (1998). *The Essential Dewey: Pragmatism, Education, Democracy*. Vol. 1. Bloomington: Indiana University Press.

Hitch, C. (1957). Letter to the Editor – Operations Research and National Planning – A Dissent. *Operations Research*, 5(5), 718–723.

Hofstadter, R. (1963). *Anti-intellectualism in American Life*. New York: Vintage Books.

Hofstede, G. (2001). *Culture's Consequences: Comparing Values, Behaviors, Institutions, and Organizations Across Nations*, 2nd ed. Beverly Hills, CA: Sage Publications.

Holling, C. S. (1986). Resilience of ecosystems; local surprise and global change. In Clark, C., and Munn, R. E., eds., *Sustainable Development of the Biosphere*. Cambridge : Cambridge University Press, pp. 292–317.

Homer-Dixon, T. (2006). *The Upside of Down: Catastrophe, Creativity, and the Renewal of Civilization*. Washington, DC: Island Press.

Hopson, R., and Cram, F. (Eds.). (2018). *Tackling Wicked Problems in Complex Ecologies: The Role of Evaluation*. Stanford, CA: Stanford University Press.

Howlett, M. (2018). Matching policy tools and their targets: Beyond nudges and utility maximisation in policy design. *Policy & Politics*, 46(1), 101–124.

Howlett, M. (2012). The lessons of failure: Learning and blame avoidance in public policy-making. *International Political Science Review*, 33(5), 539–555.

Howlett, M., Kekez, A., and Poocharoen, O. O. (2017a). Understanding co-production as a policy tool: Integrating new public governance and comparative policy theory. *Journal of Comparative Policy Analysis: Research and Practice*, 19(5), 487–501.

Howlett, M., McConnell, A., and Perl, A. (2017b). Moving policy theory forward: Connecting multiple stream and advocacy coalition frameworks to policy cycle models of analysis. *Australian Journal of Public Administration*, 76(1), 65–79.

Howlett, M., McConnell, A., and Perl, A. (2015). Streams and stages: Reconciling Kingdon and policy process theory. *European Journal of Political Research*, 54(3), 419–434.

Husted, B.W. (2005). Culture and ecology: A cross-national study of the determinants of environmental sustainability. *MIR: Management International Review*, 45(3), 349–371.

Jann, W., and Wegrich, K. (2007). Theories of the policy cycle. In Fischer, F., Miller, G. J., and Sidney, M. S., eds., *Handbook of Public Policy Analysis: Theory, Politics and Methods*. Boca Raton, FL: CRC Press, pp. 43–62.

Jenkins-Smith, H. C., and Sabatier, P. A. (1993). The study of public policy process. In Sabatier, P. A., and Jenkins-Smith, H. C., eds., *Policy and Change and Learning: An Advocacy Coalition Approach*, Boulder, CO: Westview Press. pp. 135–142.

Kay, A. (2011). Evidence-based policy-making: The elusive search for rational public administration. *Australian Journal of Public Administration*, 70(3), 236–245.

Kaufman-Osborn, T. V. (1985). Pragmatism, policy science, and the state. *American Journal of Political Science*, 4,827–849.

Kingdon, J. W., and Thurber, J. A. (1984). *Agendas, Alternatives, and Public Policies*. Boston, MA: Little, Brown.

Klein, N. (2015). *This Changes Everything: Capitalism vs. the Climate*. New York: Simon and Schuster.

Knott, J. H. (2019). The future development of schools of public policy: Five major trends. *Global Policy*, 10(1), 88–91.

Korten, D. C. (1999). *The Post-Corporate World: Life after Capitalism*. West Hartford, CT: Kumarian Press.

Korten, D. C. (1998). *When Corporations Rule the World*. West Hartford, CT: Kumarian Press.

Krastev, I. (2019). Democracy disrupted. The global politics of protest. In Randeria, S., and Wittrock, B., eds., *Social Science at the Crossroads*. Leiden, Netherlands: Brill, pp. 187–206.

Kuecker, G. D. (2020). The perfect storm's pandemic driven soft collapse. *The International Journal of Environmental, Cultural, Economic and Social Sustainability*, 16(1), 1–18.

Kuecker, G. D. (2017). Enchanting transition: A post-colonial perspective. In Henfry, T., Maschkowski, G., and Penha-Lopes, G., eds., *Resilience, Community Action, and Societal Transformation*. Hampshire, UK: Permanent Publications, pp. 193–210.

Kuecker, G. D. (2014a). A global compact? In Battersby, P., Steger, M. B., and Siracusa, J. M., eds., *The Sage Handbook of Globalization*. Vol. 2. Thousand Oaks, CA: Sage Publications, pp. 827–841.

Kuecker, G. D. (2014b). From the alienation of neoliberal globalization to transmodern ways of being: Epistemic change and the collapse of the modern world-system. *Journal of Globalization Studies*, 5(1), 154–170.

Kuecker, G. D. (2007). The perfect storm: Catastrophic collapse in the 21st century. *The International Journal of Environmental, Cultural, Economic and Social* Sustainability, 3(5), 1–10.

Kuecker, G. D. (2004). Latin American resistance movements in the time of the posts. *History Compass*, 2, 1–27.

Kuecker, G. D., and Hartley, K. (2020). Disaster risk reduction and the development narrative: Towards a new public policy epistemic. In Brik, A., and Pal, L., eds., *The Future of the Policy Sciences*. Cheltenham, UK: Edward Elgar Publishing.

Kuhn, T. (2012 [1962]). *The Structure of Scientific Revolutions*, 4th ed. Chicago: University of Chicago Press.

Lasswell, H. D. (1971a). From fragmentation to configuration. *Policy Sciences*, 2(4), 439–446.

Lasswell, H. D. (1971b). *A Pre-View of Policy Sciences*. New York: American Elsevier.

Lasswell, H. D. (1970). The emerging conception of the policy sciences. *Policy Sciences*, 1(1), 3–14.

Lasswell, H. D. (1951). The policy orientation. In Lasswell, H. D., and Lerner, D., eds., *The Policy Sciences*. Stanford, CA: Stanford University Press, pp. 3–15.

Laufer, W. S. (2003). Social accountability and corporate greenwashing. *Journal of Business Ethics*, 43(3), 253–261.

Lazer, D. M., Baum, M. A., Benkler, Y. et al. (2018). The science of fake news. *Science*, 359(6380), 1094–1096.

Levitas, R., 2013. *Utopia as Method: The Imaginary Reconstitution of Society*. New York: Palgrave Macmillan.

Li, T. M. (2007). *The Will to Improve: Governmentality, Development, and the Practice of Politics*. Durham, NC: Duke University Press.

Lindblom, C. E. (1979). Still muddling, not yet through. *Public Administration Review*, 39(6), 517–526.

Lockie, S. (2017). Post-truth politics and the social sciences. *Environmental Sociology*, 3(1), 1–5.

Lubitow, A., and Davis, M. (2011). Pastel injustice: The corporate use of pinkwashing for profit. *Environmental Justice*, 4(2), 139–144.

Lynch, K. (2015). Control by numbers: New managerialism and ranking in higher education. *Critical Studies in Education*, 56(2), 190–207.

Mallon, F. E. (1994). The promise and dilemma of subaltern studies: Perspectives from Latin American history. *The American Historical Review*, 99(5), 1491–1515.

Martin, P. (2011). *Oil in the Soil: The Politics of Paying to Preserve the Amazon*. Lanham, MD : Rowman and Littlefield.

Mas-Coma, S., Jones, M. K., and Marty, A. M. (2020). COVID-19 and globalization. *One Health*, *9*. Doi:10.1016/j.onehlt.2020.100132

McCarthy, J. (2019). Most Americans support reducing fossil fuel use. Gallup, Inc. news.gallup.com/poll/248006/americans-support-reducing-fossil-fuel.aspx

McConnell, A. (2010). *Understanding Policy Success: Rethinking Public Policy*. New York: Palgrave Macmillan.

McDougal, M. S., Lasswell, H. D., and Reisman, W. M. (1973). The intelligence function and world public order. *Temple Law Quarterly*, 46 (6), 365–448.

Meadows, D. H. (2008). *Thinking in Systems: A Primer*. White River Junction, VT: Chelsea Green Publishers.

Meadows, D. H. (1980). The unavoidable a priori. In Randers, J., ed., *Elements of the System Dynamics Method*. Cambridge, MA: Productivity Press, pp. 23–56.

Meadows, D., Randers, J., and Meadows, D. (2004). *Limits to Growth: The 30-Year Update*. White River Junction, VT: Chelsea Green Publishing Company.

Mignolo, W. (2000). *Local Histories/Global Designs: Coloniality, Subaltern Knowledge, and Border Thinking*. Princeton, NJ: Princeton University Press.

Mukhtarov, F., and Gerlak, A. K. (2014). Epistemic forms of integrated water resources management: Towards knowledge versatility. *Policy Sciences*, 47(2), 101–120.

Murphy, R. (2012). Sustainability: A wicked problem. *Sociologica* 2.

Noble, S. U. (2018). *Algorithms of Oppression: How Search Engines Reinforce Racism*. New York: New York University Press.

O'Neil, C. (2016). *Weapons of Math Destruction: How Big Data Increases Inequality and Threatens Democracy*. New York: Broadway Books.

Orach, K., and Schlüter, M. (2016). Uncovering the political dimension of social-ecological systems: Contributions from policy process frameworks. *Global Environmental Change*, 40,13–25.

Oreskes, N., and Conway, E. M. (2013). The collapse of Western civilization: A view from the future. *Daedalus*, 142(1), 40–58.

Ostrom, E. (2011). Background on the institutional analysis and development framework. *Policy Studies Journal*, 39(1), 7–27.

Peters, B. G. (2018). *Policy problems and policy design.* Cheltenham, UK: Edward Elgar Publishing.

Peters, B. G. (2017). What is so wicked about wicked problems? A conceptual analysis and a research program. *Policy and Society*, 36(3), 385–396.

Peters, B. G. (2005). The problem of policy problems. *Journal of Comparative Policy Analysis*, 7(4), 349–370.

Pollitt, C. (2007). The new public management: An overview of its current status. *Administration and Public Management Review*, 8,110–115.

Porpora, D., and Sekalala, S. (2019). Truth, communication, and democracy. *International Journal of Communication*, 13,18.

Price, M. F. (1990). Humankind in the biosphere: The evolution of international interdisciplinary research. *Global Environmental Change*, 1(1), 3–13.

Pryshlakivsky, J., and Searcy, C. (2013). Sustainable development as a wicked problem. In Kovacic, S. F., and Sousa-Poza, A., eds., *Managing and Engineering in Complex Situations*. Dordrecht: Springer Netherlands, pp. 109–128.

Ripple, W. J., Wolf, C., Newsome, T. M., Barnard, P., and Moomaw, W. R. (2020). World scientists' warning of a climate emergency. *BioScience*, 70(1), 8–12.

Rittel, H., and Weber, M. (1973). Dilemmas in a general theory of planning. *Policy Sciences*, 4(2), 155–169.

Rodrik, D. (2018). Populism and the economics of globalization. *Journal of International Business Policy*, 1(1–2), 12–33.

Room, G. (2011). *Complexity, Institutions and Public Policy: Agile Decision-Making in a Turbulent World*. Cheltenham, UK: Edward Elgar Publishing.

Sabatier, P. A., and Jenkins-Smith, H. (1993). *Policy Change and Learning: An Advocacy Coalition Approach*. Boulder, CO: Westview Press.

Said, E. W. (1979). *Orientalism*. New York: Vintage.

Satterthwaite, D. (2001). From professionally driven to people-driven poverty reduction: Reflections on the role of Shack/Slum Dwellers International. *Environment and Urbanization*, 13(2), 135–138.

Schlager, E. (1999). A comparison of frameworks, theories, and models of policy processes. In Sabatier, P., ed., *Theories of the Policy Process*. Boulder, CO: Westview Press, pp. 233–260.

Schmidt, N. M., and Fleig, A. (2018). Global patterns of national climate policies: Analyzing 171 country portfolios on climate policy integration. *Environmental Science and Policy*, 84,177–185.

Scott, J. C. (1998). *Seeing like a State: How Certain Schemes to Improve the Human Condition Have Failed.* New Haven, CT: Yale University Press.

Sen, A. K. (1977). Rational fools: A critique of the behavioral foundations of economic theory. *Philosophy & Public Affairs,* 6(4), 317–344.

Shiva, V. (2010). Making peace with the earth. City of Sydney Peace Prize Lecture. Sydney Opera House, Sydney, Australia. November 3, https:// sydneypeacefoundation.org.au/wp-content/uploads/2012/02/2010-SPP_ Vandana-Shiva.pdf

Smith, L. T. (2012). *Decolonizing Methodologies: Research and Indigenous Peoples.* London : Zed Books.

Steelman, T. (2016). US wildfire governance as social-ecological problem. *Ecology and Society,* 21(4), 3.

Suiter, J. (2016). Post-truth politics. *Political Insight,* 7(3), 25–27.

Svara, J. H. (2008). Beyond dichotomy: Dwight Waldo and the intertwined politics-administration relationship. *Public Administration Review,* 68(1), 46–52.

Taylor, F. W. (1911). The principles of scientific management. Reprinted in Taylor, F. W., ed., (1964), *Scientific Management.* London : Harper & Row.

Taylor, M. (2001). *The Moment of Complexity: Emerging Network Culture.* Chicago: University of Chicago Press.

Tenbensel, T. (2006). Policy knowledge for policy work. In Colebatch, H. K., ed., *The Work of Policy: An International Survey.* New York: Lexington Books, pp. 199–216.

Tuck, E., and Yang, K. W. (2012). Decolonization is not a metaphor. *Decolonization: Indigeneity, Education & Society,* 1(1), 1–40.

Turnbull, N. (2006). How should we theorise public policy? Problem solving and problematicity. *Policy and Society,* 25(2), 3–22.

Tyfield, D. (2012). A cultural political economy of research and innovation in an age of crisis. *Minerva,* 50(2), 149–167.

van Beek, U., Fuchs, D., and Klingemann, H. D. (2019). The question of legitimacy in contemporary democracies. In Van Beck, U., ed., *Democracy Under Threat: A Crisis of Legitimacy?* Cham, Switzerland: Palgrave Macmillan, pp. 321–335.

Waldo, D. (1952). Development of theory of democratic administration. *American Political Science Review,* 46(1), 81–103.

Waldrop, M. M. (1992). *Complexity: The Emerging Science at the Edge of Order and Chaos.* New York: Simon and Schuster.

Walker, B. H., and Salt, D. A. (2006). *Resilience Thinking Sustaining Ecosystems and People in a Changing World.* Washington, DC: Island Press.

Weber, M. (1978 [1921]). *Economy and Society: An Outline of Interpretive Sociology.* Berkeley: University of California Press.

Westley, F. R., Tjornbo, O., Schultz, L., Olsson, P., Folke, C., Crona, B., and Bodin, Ö. (2013). A theory of transformative agency in linked social-ecological systems. *Ecology and Society,* 18(3), 27.

Whitworth, J. (2020). COVID-19: A fast evolving pandemic. *Transactions of The Royal Society of Tropical Medicine and Hygiene,* 114(4), 241.

Ye, Z., Yang, J., Zhong, N., Tu, X., Jia, J., and Wang, J. (2020). Tackling environmental challenges in pollution controls using artificial intelligence: A review. *Science of The Total Environment,* 699,134279.

Zahariadis, N. (2007). The multiple streams framework: Structure, limitations, prospects. In Sabatier, P., ed., *Theories of the Policy Process.* Boulder, CO: Westview Press, pp. 65–92.

Zuboff, S. (2019). *The Age of Surveillance Capitalism: The Fight for a Human Future at the New Frontier of Power.* New York: Public Affairs.

Glossary

Common sense:
: The unquestioned and indisputable acceptance of ways of being, thinking, and acting that do not require intentionality in their routine performance.

Complexity:
: A highly ordered system that is often self-organizing, emergent, evolving, and governed by a rule set that emerged endogenously from the random interactions of constituent elements.

Enlightenment thinking:
: A legacy of policy thinking emerging from the historical Enlightenment that dictates epistemic terms according to a largely unchallenged empiricist perspective. This way of thinking is also credited with placing the individual and individual interests at the center of efforts to understand society and policy, bearing implications for how policy understands and anticipates human behavior.

Hegemony:
: The dominance enjoyed by one idea or practice relative to others, often serving particular social or economic interests and maintained through an institutional architecture designed to protect those interests.

Instrumental rationalism:
: The thought-system and accompanying rule set holding that discrete and targeted olicy interventions (as instruments or tools) can be successfully applied to problems expressed in knowable and well-defined terms. We use the term instrumental rationalism, as against instrumental rationality, in reference to a normative logic around which the policy profession structures its analytical thinking. If rationality is the act of being rational, rationalism is the epistemic rule set and belief system that institutionalizes rationality.

Intelligence function:
: As understood by the field of policy sciences, the constellation of institutions, actors, resources, and epistemic orientations that constitute society's capacity to attempt to measure, understand, and solve policy problems.

Legacy thinking:	Ways of thinking about public policy that fail to acknowledge fully and appropriately the contextual realities of the twenty-first century; examples are Enlightenment rationalism and instrumental rationalism.
Liminality/problem of transition:	The period of time in the transition between system states when the state of the system is indeterminant. During this period of instability, old epistemics have lost their credibility and hegemonic status but no alternative epistemic has emerged to occupy the void.
Modernity:	The period in which an Enlightenment-rationalist way of viewing and practicing public policy was hegemonic.
Other knowledges:	Ways of understanding reality and acting on those understandings that have been historically marginalized in service to hegemonic epistemics (e.g., Enlightenment rationalism and instrumental rationalism).
Paradigm shift:	The transition from a hegemonic epistemic to another epistemic or to a state without a hegemonic epistemic.
Perfect storm:	The presence of convergent and interdependent crises, wicked problems, and epistemic uncertainty that characterizes the context in which public policy operates in the twenty-first century. In its advanced state, complexity reveals an epistemic fluidity in which old ways of thinking are anachronistic but new ways of thinking are not fully formed or understood.
Policy epistemic:	The logic of thought underlying commonly understood practices and structures of public policy, often shaped by ideas emerging from power struggles and by the self-serving narratives promoted by victors of those struggles.
Power-knowledge nexus:	A sociopolitical community in which the producers of knowledge (e.g., global development institutions, think tanks, consultancies, academics, and other self-referential experts) operate in service to elite political and economic

constituencies, supporting hegemonic narratives that marginalize challenges to system properties that protect powerful interests.

Predicament thinking: "The acknowledgment by policy practitioners that policy should not obsess over solutions to discrete problems but should instead acknowledge the need to live with and manage the impacts of problems that are wicked and unsolvable" (Hartley, Kuecker, and Woo 2019, p. 164).

Public policy: The step between what needs to be done and the actual doing; a translation between thought and the "real world" where policy provides instructions, guardrails, and rule sets. This translation occurs within the context of actors, ideas, and institutions that shape content and mediate implementation. As policy produces, sustains, and reproduces itself and its rule sets, it emerges as one of several determinants of power relations and influences how social, political, economic, and cultural practices become hegemonic forms of common sense.

Soft collapse: A system's movement from ordered complexity toward disordered simplicity, during which the integrity of system complexity is not entirely lost while the system, to some extent, enters a liminal state with an uncertain outcome. During a soft collapse, failures of the hegemonic epistemic and its policy manifestations produce observable systemic destabilization and decline. Defenders of the hegemonic epistemic respond by doubling-down on legacy modes of thinking while defending their credibility against an onslaught of anomalous data and political pushback. The doubling-down results in momentary but illusory resolution of policy problems without progress on underlying determinants. The temporarily successful state ultimately gives way to an eventual hard collapse.

Technocracy: A way of understanding and practicing public policy that privileges the truth claims and rule sets of empiricist and rationalist epistemics, as constituted and sanctioned by experts holding specialized knowledge that aligns with privileged truth claims and rule sets.

Wicked problems: Policy problems whose characteristics and causes are mutable and difficult to measure, and whose solutions are unclear, beyond the reach of policy, or nonexistent.

Cambridge Elements ☰

Public Policy

M. Ramesh
National University of Singapore (NUS)
M. Ramesh is UNESCO Chair on Social Policy Design at the Lee Kuan Yew School of Public Policy, NUS. His research focuses on governance and social policy in East and Southeast Asia, in addition to public policy institutions and processes. He has published extensively in reputed international journals. He is Co-editor of Policy and Society and Policy Design and Practice.

Michael Howlett
Simon Fraser University, British Columbia
Michael Howlett is Burnaby Mountain Professor and Canada Research Chair (Tier 1) in the Department of Political Science, Simon Fraser University. He specialises in public policy analysis, and resource and environmental policy. He is currently editor-in-chief of *Policy Sciences* and co-editor of the *Journal of Comparative Policy Analysis; Policy and Society* and *Policy Design and Practice.*

Xun WU
Hong Kong University of Science and Technology
Xun WU is Professor and Head of the Division of Public Policy at the Hong Kong University of Science and Technology. He is a policy scientist whose research interests include policy innovations, water resource management and health policy reform. He has been involved extensively in consultancy and executive education, his work involving consultations for the World Bank and UNEP.

Judith Clifton
University of Cantabria
Judith Clifton is Professor of Economics at the University of Cantabria, Spain. She has published in leading policy journals and is editor-in-chief of the *Journal of Economic Policy Reform*. Most recently, her research enquires how emerging technologies can transform public administration, a forward-looking cutting-edge project which received €3.5 million funding from the Horizon2020 programme.

Eduardo Araral
National University of Singapore (NUS)
Eduardo Araral is widely published in various journals and books and has presented in forty conferences. He is currently Co-Director of the Institute of Water Policy at the Lee Kuan Yew School of Public Policy, NUS and is a member of the editorial board of *Journal of Public Administration Research and Theory* and the board of the Public Management Research Association.

About the Series
Elements in Public Policy is a concise and authoritative collection of assessments of the state of the art and future research directions in public policy research, as well as substantive new research on key topics. Edited by leading scholars in the field, the series is an ideal medium for reflecting on and advancing the understanding of critical issues in the public sphere. Collectively, the series provides a forum for broad and diverse coverage of all major topics in the field while integrating different disciplinary and methodological approaches.

Cambridge Elements ≡

Public Policy

Elements in the series

Printed in the United States
by Baker & Taylor Publisher Services

Printed in the United States
by Baker & Taylor Publisher Services